SHOW CAVES IN SLOVAKIA
SCHAUHÖHLEN DER SLOWAKEI

© 1997 KNIŽNÉ CENTRUM, vydavateľstvo
Predmestská 51, 010 01 Žilina
for Správa slovenských jaskýň, Liptovský Mikuláš
Authors: RNDr. Pavel Bella (text), Miroslav Eliáš (photo),
Ing. Ján Kasák (graphic design)
Translation: Štefan Straka (English), Helena Grofčíková (German)
Editor: Bohuslav Kortman
Litho: M&P Žilina. Print: Žilinské tlačiarne, a. s., Žilina

ISBN 80-88723-52-3

SHOW CAVES IN SLOVAKIA   SCHAUHÖHLEN DER SLOWAKEI

The caves are real gems of the Nature, adornments of nature and of the people who discovered them. Rockscape, strange effects of water, distinctive underground shapes and fillings, special climate, findings of human settlement and old relics of mankind, remains of animals from very long ago, as well as the present time fauna - that is the manysided, and for most of us mysterious world of caves.

Great number of caves in a relatively small area in the heart of Europe, their irreplaceable natural-historical and aesthetic value make Slovakia a speleological power of world importance.

We appreciate the efforts of generations of explorers who were discovering and exploring in hard conditions these diamonds of nature for the sake of mankind. Doing so, many lost their health and often also their lives.

Caves as irreplaceable natural values require constant care and thorough protection. This is particularly true about the show caves open to the public. It is essential for every visitor to the caves to become aware of it.

The ultimate goal of the authors of this publication is to draw nearer the readers and other interested people from Slovakia and from abroad to the show caves in Slovakia, by means of descriptions, and, first of all, by picture. I strongly believe that all the readers will find here adequate pieces of information and will like it.

Last but not least, the authors sincerely wish that each visit to the Slovak caves will be an unforgettable experience for the visitor and a tribute paid to the unfathomable and graceful Mother Nature.

Die Höhlen sind wahre Kleinoden der Natur. Sie sind Zierden der Natur und der Menschen, die sie entdeckten. Gesteine, ungewöhnliche Wasserwirkung, eigenartige unterirdische Formationen und Ausfüllungen, besonderes Klima, Besiedlungsnachweise und Spuren der Menschen, Überreste von Tieren aus der weiten Vergangenheit und die jetzige Fauna bilden die bunte und für die meisten von uns geheimnisvolle Mosaik der Höhlenwelt.

Ungewöhnlich große Häufigkeit der Höhlen auf dem relativ kleinen Territorium im Herzen Europas, ihre unwiederholbaren naturwissenschaftlichen und ästhetischen Werte machen aus der Slowakischen Republik ein Höhlenland mit weltweiter Bedeutung.

Wir schätzen die Bemühungen ganzer Forschergenerationen, welche diese Juwelen der Natur in schwierigen Bedingungen entdeckten und kennenlernten. Viele kamen dabei um ihre Gesundheit und manche auch ums Leben.

Höhlen als unersetzbare Naturwerte bedürfen ständiger Pflege und gründlichen Schutzes. Dies betrifft besonders die der Öffentlichkeit zugänglichen Höhlen. Wichtig ist, daß es jedem Besucher der Höhle bewußt wird.

Die Absicht der Verfasser dieser Publikation ist, mit Wort, aber vor allem mit Bild die Schauhöhlen der Slowakei ihren Besuchern und anderen in- und ausländischen Interessenten etwas näher zu bringen. Ich hoffe, daß hier jeder die notwendigen Informationen findet und daß unsere Höhlen allen gefallen werden.

Wir können uns wünschen, daß jede Besichtigung der Schauhöhle in uns ein unvergeßliches Erlebnis hinterläßt. Bezeigen wir der ungewöhnlichen und gnädigen Natur unsere Ehre!

Jozef Hlaváč
director
Administration of the Slovak Caves

Jozef Hlaváč
Direktor
Slowakische Höhlenverwaltung

KARST TERRITORIES AND CAVES IN SLOVAKIA

Karst territories are characteristic by their distinctive geomorphological and hydrological phenomena (lapies, dolines, schratten fields, blind and half-blind valleys, gorges, canyons, caves, ponors, underground streams and pools, karst springs etc.) created by chemical dissolving of limestones or soluble rocks. They cover more than 2,700 sq. km in Slovakia and represent the important landscape entities of the Western Carpathians.

Following kinds of karst are represented in the temperate climatic zone of Central Europe: plateau karst (Slovak Karst, Muránska Plateau, Slovak Paradise), karst of massive ridges, horsts and combined fold-fault structures (Strážovské Hills, Lesser Carpathians, Starohorské Hills), dissected karst of monoclinal crests and ridges (Low Tatras, Greater Fatra), to a less extent karst of klippen structure (Vršatské Clippen in the White Carpathians, Manín, Pieniny), karst of travertine domes and cascades (Dreveník in the Hornád Basin), karst of isolated blocks and monadnocks, and karst of foothill plains and terraces (Horná Lehota Karst in the Upper Hron River Valley).

There is also some representation of high-mountain karst (Red Hills in the Western Tatras, the highest elevations of the Belianske Tatras and High Tatras). Cryptokarst related to lens-shaped formation of crystalline limestones in the basement of impervious rocks (Ochtinský Cryptokarst, in the Revúcka Highland) is of special importance.

More than 3,800 caves are known in Slovakia, most of them situated in the Slovak Karst, Low Tatras, Spiš-Gemer Karst (Slovak Paradise, Muránska Plateau), Greater Fatra, Western Tatras, High Tatras and Belianske Tatras.

The system of the Demänovská caves in the Low Tatras is the most extensive one, reaching the length of about 24 km. The system of Stratenská cave - Psie

diery (Dog Holes) in the Slovak Paradise is 21.5 km long. The cave Starý hrad (Old Castle) in the Low Tatras is 432 m deep, the cave Javorinka in the High Tatras is 320 m deep and the Javorová priepasť (Maple Chasm) in the Low Tatras is 312 m deep.

Permanent ice filling is in 39 caves. Unique decoration can be found in the Ochtinská Aragonite Cave in the Revúcka Highland. According to the Guiness Book of Records the highest stalagmite in the world (32.4 m) is in the Krásnohorská Cave in the Silická Plateau in the Slovak Karst. Rich findings of bones of vertebrates are characteristic for the caves Medvedia (Bear) and Psie diery in the Slovak Paradise.

The caves with their mysteries have been attracting attention of man since time immemorial. Some of them were for some time inhabited by man or were used as hiding places or shelters. Among important archaeological sites rank the Ardovská Cave, Domica Cave, Majda-Hraškova Cave (Slovak Karst), Veľká ružinska Cave (Black Mountain), Prepoštská

Cave (Prievidzská Basin), Devil's Oven Cave (Považský Inovec mountains), Hollow Rock Cave and Dark Rock Cave (Lesser Carpathians), and others. Remarkable inscriptions have been preserved on the walls of several caves. During the World War II many caves served as shelters.

According to the Act of the National Council of Slovak Republic - No. 287/1994 of the Law Digest - On the Protection of Nature and Landscape, all the caves should be considered nature monuments and educational localities. Thirty caves and chasms have been designated national nature monuments. The joint Slovak-Hungarian project „Caves of the Slovak and Aggtelek Karst" was included to the list of the World Natural Heritage in December 1995.

Every year new cave spaces would be discovered,

mostly thanks to voluntary speleologists associated in the Slovak Speleological Society.

A whole-Slovakia office - The Administration of the Slovak Caves, as well as a specialised Slovak Museum of Nature Protection and Speleology is situated in the city of Liptovský Mikuláš.

KARST UND HÖHLEN DER SLOWAKEI

Die Karstgebiete sind durch eigenartige geomorphologische und hydrologische Erscheinungen (Karren, Dolinen, Uvalas, Blind- und Halbblindtäler, Canons, Höhlen, Wasserschwinden, unterirdische Flüsse und Seen, Karstquellen etc.) gekennzeichnet, die durch chemische Auflösung der Kalksteine oder anderer löslicher Gesteine entstehen. In der Slowakei nehmen sie die Fläche von mehr als 2700 km^2 ein und stellen bedeutsame Landschaftsgebiete der Westlichen Karpaten dar.

In der milden Klimazone Mitteleuropas sind vertreten der Plateaukarst (Slovenský kras, Muránska planina, Slovenský raj), der Karst der massiven Bergrücken, Horste und kombinierten Falten-Bruch-Strukturen (Strážovské vrchy, Kleine Karpaten, Starohorské vrchy), der zergliederte Karst der monoklinen Bergkämme und Bergrücken (Niedere Tatra, Große Fatra), im kleineren Ausmaß der Karst der Klippenstruktur (Vršatecké bradlá in den Weißen Karpaten, Manín, Pieniny), der Karst der Travertinkuppen und -kaskaden (Dreveník in Hornádska kotlina), der Karst der isolierten Schollen und Härtlinge, der Karst der Bergfußplateaus und -terassen (Hornolehotský kras in Horehronské podolie).

Ebenso kommt auch der Hochgebirgskarst vor (Červené vrchy in der Westlichen Tatra, höchste Lagen von Belianske Tatry und von der Hohen Tatra). Besondere Bedeutung hat der sich an die Linsen der Kristallkalksteine im Unterbau der undurchlässigen Gesteine bindende Kryptokarst (Ochtinský kryptokras in Revúcka vrchovina).

In der Slowakei sind mehr als 3800 Höhlen bekannt. Die meisten davon sind in Slovenský kras, in der Niederen Tatra, in Spišsko-gemerský kras (Slovenský raj, Muránska planina), in der Großen Fatra, in der Westlichen und der Hohen Tatra und in Belianske Tatry.

Das System der Demänová-Höhlen in der Niederen Tatra von etwa 24 km Länge ist am umfangreichsten. Das Höhlensystem Stratenská jaskyňa - Psie diery in Slovenský raj ist 21,5 km lang. Die Höhle Starý hrad in der Niederen Tatra ist 432 m tief, die Höhle Javorinka in der Hohen Tatra 320 m und Javorová priepasť in der Niederen Tatra ist 312 m tief.

39 Höhlen sind andauernd vereist. Sehr einzigartige Dekoration gibt es in der Aragonithöhle Ochtiná in Revúcka vrchovina. Der laut dem Guiness-Buch höchste Stalagmit in der Welt (32,4 m) befindet sich in der Höhle Krásnohorská jaskyňa in Silická planina in Slovenský kras. Durch reiche Entdeckungen an Wirbeltierenknochen sind die Höhlen Medvedia jaskyňa und Psie diery in Slovenský raj charakteristisch.

Seit langer Zeit ziehen die geheimnisvollen Höhlen die Aufmerksamkeit der Menschen an. Einige davon waren eine Zeitlang besiedelt oder wurden als Versteck oder Wohnhöhlen genutzt. Zu den bedeutsamen archäologischen Fundorten gehören die Höhlen Ardovská jaskyňa, Domica, Majda-Hraškova jaskyňa (Slovenský kras), Veľká ružínska jaskyňa (Čierna hora), Prepoštská jaskyňa (Prievidzská kotlina), Čertova pec (Považský Inovec), Deravá skala und Tmavá skala (Kleine Karpaten) u.a. An den Wänden von mehreren Höhlen sind beachtenswerte Aufschriften erhalten geblieben. Während des 2. Weltkrieges dienten viele Höhlen als Verstecke.

Gemäß dem Gesetz des Nationalrates der Slowakischen Republik Nr. 287/1994 über Natur- und Landschaftsschutz werden alle Höhlen als Naturdenkmäler und Lehrgebiete betrachtet. 30 Höhlen und Abgrunde wurden zu nationalen Naturdenkmälern erklärt. Das bilaterale slowakisch-ungarische Projekt „Höhlen des Slowakischen und Aggtelekerschen Karstes" wurde im Dezember 1995 in die Naturerbe-Weltliste aufgenommen.

Jedes Jahr werden neue Höhlen entdeckt, vor allem dank den freiwilligen Speläologen aus der Slowakischen Speläologie-Gesellschaft. In Liptovský Mikuláš haben die Slowakische Höhlenverwaltung sowie das Museum für Naturschutz und Speläologie ihren Sitz.

SHOW CAVES IN SLOVAKIA

Twelve caves have been made public in Slovakia to date. Their appropriate and optimal utilisation rests in monitoring of impact of the rate of visitors on natural environment of caves, including its regulation. All the show caves are designated national nature monuments.

The Ochtinská Aragonite Cave, Domica Cave, Gombasecká Cave and Jasovská Cave have been included in the World Natural Heritage since 1995. As priceless and unique values of the international importance they deserve special protection, care and publicity.

Protection and maintenance of the show caves in Slovakia are under the responsibility of the Administration of the Slovak Caves in Liptovský Mikuláš - a qualified institution of nature protection of the Ministry of the Environment of the Slovak Republic.

SCHAUHÖHLEN DER SLOWAKEI

In der Slowakei gibt es zwölf Schauhöhlen. Ihre angemessene und optimale Nützung basiert auf der Beobachtung des Einflusses der Besichtigungen auf das natürliche Höhlenmilieu sowie auf deren Optimierung. Alle Schauhöhlen sind nationale Naturdenkmäler.

Die Höhlen Ochtinská aragonitová jaskyňa, Domica, Gombasecká jaskyňa und Jasovská jaskyňa gehören seit 1995 zum Weltnaturerbe. Als unschätzbare und unersetzbare Werte mit weltweiter Bedeutung bedürfen sie besonderen Schutzes, Pflege sowie Präsentation.

Der Schutz und der Betrieb der slowakischen Schauhöhlen wird von der Slowakischen Höhlenverwaltung in Liptovský Mikuláš als einer für Naturschutz spezialisierten Organisation des slowakischen Umweltministeriums vorgenommen.

Name of the Cave / Höhle	Open for the public / Betriebszeit	Length of the show tour / Länge der Besichtigungsroute	Duration of the guided tour / Besichtigungsdauer
Belianska jaskyňa	1.1.–15.11. 1.12.–31.12.	1275 m	70 min.
Bystrianska jaskyňa	1.1.–31.10.	545 m	45 min.
Demänovská jaskyňa slobody	1.1.–31.10. 1.12.–31.12.	A – 1145 m B – 2150 m	60 min. 100 min.
Demänovská ľadová jaskyňa	15.5.–15.9.	850 m	45 min.
Dobšinská ľadová jaskyňa	15.5.–15.9.	515 m	40 min.
Domica	1.2.–31.12.	A – 780 m B – 1560 m	45 min. 85 min.
Driny	1.4.–31.10.	450 m	35 min.
Gombasecká jaskyňa	1.4.–31.10.	530 m	35 min.
Harmanecká jaskyňa	1.5.–31.10.	1020 m	80 min.
Jasovská jaskyňa	1.4.–31.10.	720 m	45 min.
Ochtinská aragonitová jaskyňa	1.4.–31.10.	585 m	45 min.
Važecká jaskyňa	1.2.–30.11.	325 m	35 min.

BELIANSKA JASKYŇA

NATIONAL NATURE MONUMENT
NATIONALES NATURDENKMAL

Cadastral area/
Katastergebiet:
Tatranská Lomnica
District/Kreis:
Poprad
Region/Bezirk:
Prešov

THE BELIANSKA CAVE

Situated on the northern slopes of Kobylí vrch (Mare Hill) in the eastern part of the Belianske Tatras, near the village Tatranská Kotlina, in the National Nature Reserve Belianske Tatras in the territory of the Tatra National Park. Entrance to the cave is 890 m a.s.l.

It was created in the Middle Triassic Gutenstein limestones of the Krížňanský nappe by the waters penetrating along interbed surfaces and tectonic faults. Total cave length is 1,752 m and vertical range is 160 m.

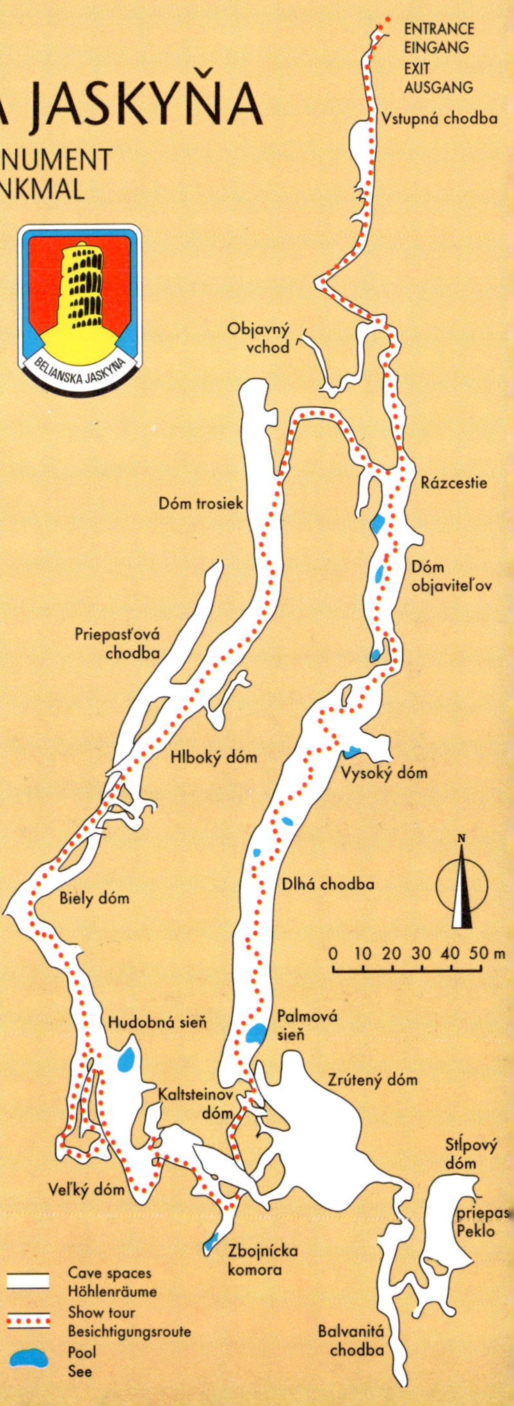

The entrance parts are open by a thirled tunnel. Chimney spaces from the upper, original entrance, which was situated 82 m above the present one, infall in them. Ascending and descending parts of the show route are locally extended into dome and hall spaces. Forms of water modelling have been preserved in several parts of the cave. A noticeable vertical dissection of the cave is shaped also by chasms.

Sinter „waterfalls", pagoda-like stalagmites and several sinter pools are very attractive. Also other forms of sinter filling are richly represented.

Front parts of the cave were known to gold miners as late as in the first half of the 18th century. However, for long years to come the rest of the cave remained hidden to man's eyes. In 1881, the cave was entered by J. Husz and J. Britz. The discoveries in 1881 and 1882 were shared by A. Kaltstein, I. Verbovszky and J. Britz. A part of the cave has been open to the public as early as since 1882. Electric lights were installed in 1896. The Hudobná sieň (Music Hall) serves for concerts. Currently accessible are 1,135 m.

DIE HÖHLE BELIANSKA

Die Höhle befindet sich auf dem Nordabhang des Berges Kobylí vrch im östlichen Teil vom Gebirgszug Belianske Tatry über der Gemeinde Tatranská Kotlina. Sie liegt in der Nationalen Naturreservation Belianske Tatry auf dem Gebiet des Tatra-Nationalparks. Der Eingang in die Höhle liegt 890 m ü. d. M.

Die Höhle ist in mitteltriassischen Gutensteinkalken der Krížna-Decke vom Schnee- und Eiswasser oder von starken Niederschlägen gebildet worden, die Schichtenzwischenflächen und tektonische Störungen entlang durchsickerten. Die Höhle ist 1752 m lang, mit Höhenunterschied von 160 m.

Die Eintrittsteile wurden durch ein Tunell zugänglich gemacht. Hier münden Kaminräume von dem oberen, ursprünglichen Eingang, der 82 m über dem jetzigen Eingang liegt. Die Auf- und Abstiegsteile der Besichtigungsroute erweitern sich manchmal in Dom- und Saalräume. An mehreren Stellen sind Formen der Wassermodellierung erhalten geblieben. Die Höhle ist vertikal durch zahlreiche Schluchten gegliedert.

Interessant sind hier die Sinterwasserfälle, pagodenförmige Stalagmiten und mehrere kleine Seen. Auch andere Formen der Sinterausfüllung sind reichlich vertreten.

Die vorderen Teile der Höhle waren den Goldgräbern bereits in der ersten Hälfte des 18. Jahrhunderts bekannt. Lange Jahre blieb sie jedoch verborgen. 1881 traten in die Höhle J. Husz und J. Britz ein. An den Entdeckungen in den Jahren 1881 und 1882 beteiligten sich A. Kaltstein, I. Verbovszky und J. Britz. Ein Teil der Höhle wurde bereits seit 1882 erschlossen. Seit 1896 ist diese Höhle elektrisch beleuchtet. Im Hudobná sieň (Musiksaal) finden die Konzerte statt. Gegenwärtig sind 1135 m der Höhle erschlossen.

BYSTRIANSKA JASKYŇA
NATIONAL NATURE MONUMENT
NATIONALES NATURDENKMAL

Cadastral area/Katastergebiet: Bystrá, Valaská
District/Kreis: Brezno
Region/Bezirk: Banská Bystrica

THE BYSTRIANSKA CAVE

Situated in the Bystrá-Valaská Karst in the Upper Hron River Valley, at the southern border of Bystrá village in Tále tourist resort, on the southern slopes of the Low Tatras. Entrance to the cave is at the foothill of the north-western slopes of Chodorov Hill, 565 m a.s.l.

It was formed in Middle Triassic limestones of the Chočský nappe along the tectonic faults by underground waters of Bystrianka stream which flows to the karst territory from the southern slopes of the Low Tatras. It consists of the Old and the New Cave, about 2,000 m in length, with vertical range of 92 m. Shapes of river modelling are richly represented.

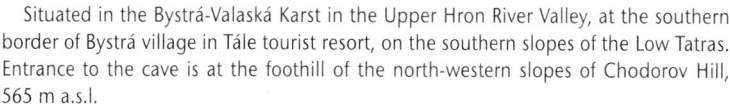

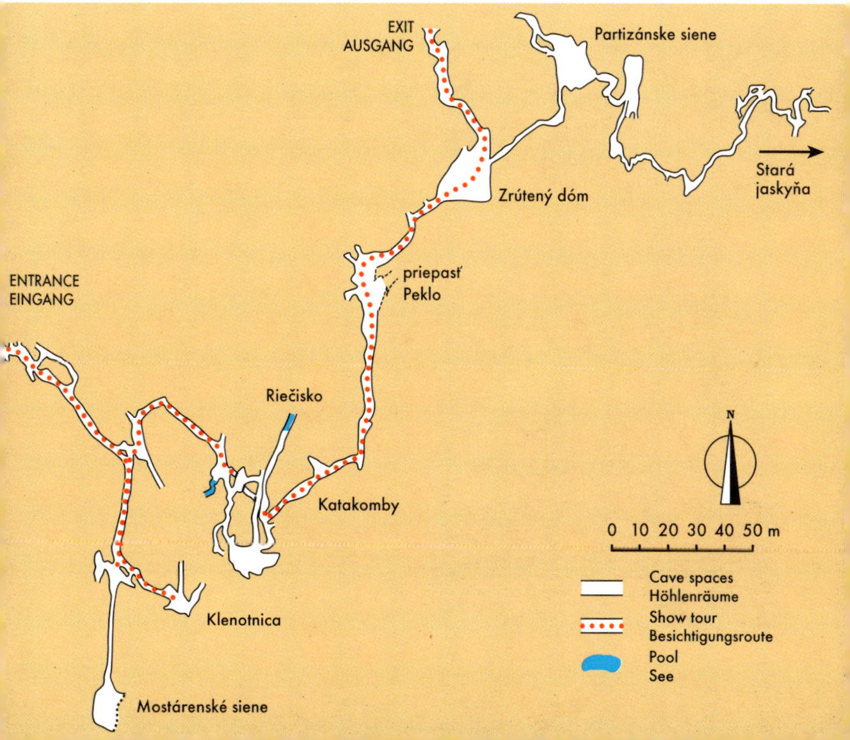

Draperies, hanging locally from the edges of sinter crusts created on the former river sediments which were later floated by the river, prevail among sinter filling.

Opening to the Old Cave was known to the locals since the ancient times. Farther spaces were discovered in 1923 by J. Kovalčík and E. Laubert. The chasm Peklo (Hell) through which the access to the New Cave was later found, was discovered by E. and A. Hollmann and J. Kovalčík, in 1926. A part of the cave was made public in 1939 and 1940. Tragic events of anti-Fascist resistance during the World War II are commemorated by a memorial tablet. The current 490 m of cave spaces have been made public in 1968. It has been serving for speleotherapeutic procedures since 1972.

DIE HÖHLE BYSTRIANSKA

Die Höhle befindet sich im Karstgebiet Bystriansko-valaštiansky kras in Horehronské podolie am südlichen Rande der Gemeinde Bystrá in der Nähe des Erholungszentrums Tále auf dem Südabhang der Niederen Tatra. Der Eingang in die Höhle auf dem nordwestlichen Abhang des Berges Chodorov vrch liegt 565 m ü. d. M.

Sie ist in mitteltriassischen Kalksteinen der Choč-Decke den tektonischen Störungen vom unterirdischen Gewässer des kleinen Flusses Bystrianka entlang gebildet worden, der in das Karstgebiet aus den südlichen Hängen der Niederen Tatra zufließt. Die Höhle besteht aus der Alten und der Neuen Höhle, ihre Länge beträgt ca. 2000 m und die vertikale Spannweite beträgt ca. 92 m. Eine bedeutsame Vertretung haben hier die Gebilde der Fluß-Modellierung.

In der Sinterausfüllung sind Vorhänge dominierend, die an einigen Stellen aus dem oberen Rand der Sinterkrusten hängen, die auf den ehemaligen, später abgeschwemmten Fluß-Sedimenten gebildet worden sind.

Die Öffnung in die Alte Höhle war den örtlichen Einwohnern seit langem bekannt. Weitere Teile der Höhle wurden 1923 von J. Kovalčík und E. Laubert entdeckt. Die Schlucht Peklo (Hölle), durch die dann später die Neue Höhle erschlossen wurde, wurde 1926 von E. u. A. Hollmann und J. Kovalčík entdeckt. Ein Teil der Höhle wurde 1939 und 1940 für die Öffentlichkeit zugänglich gemacht. An ein tragisches Ereignis aus dem antifaschistischen Kampf im 2. Weltkrieg erinnert die Andenktafel. Im jetzigen Zustand ist die Höhle für die Öffentlichkeit seit 1968 mit einer Länge von 490 m zugänglich. Seit 1972 wird die Höhle für Speläotherapie genützt.

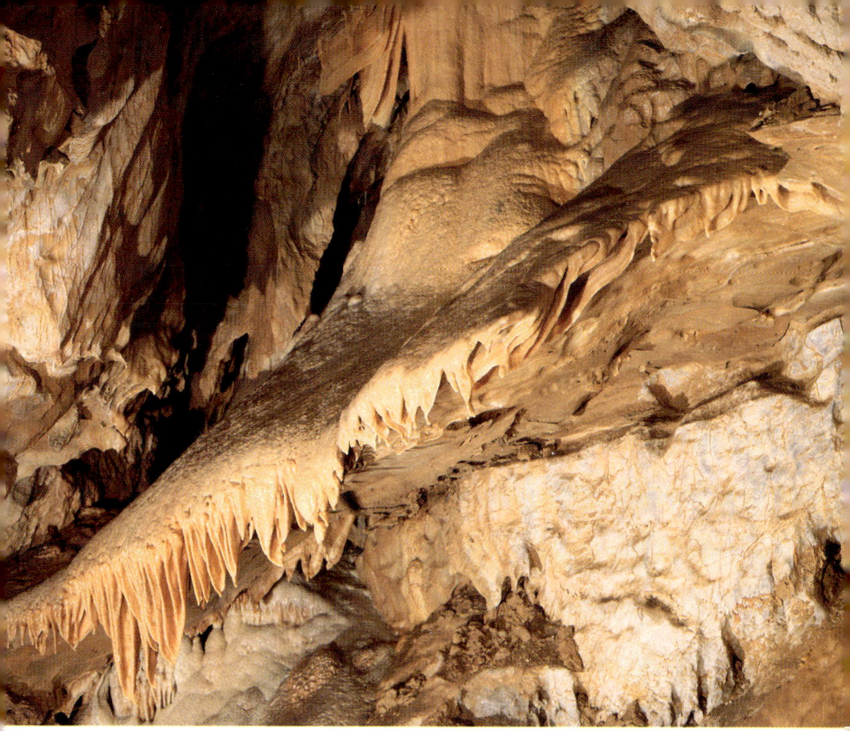

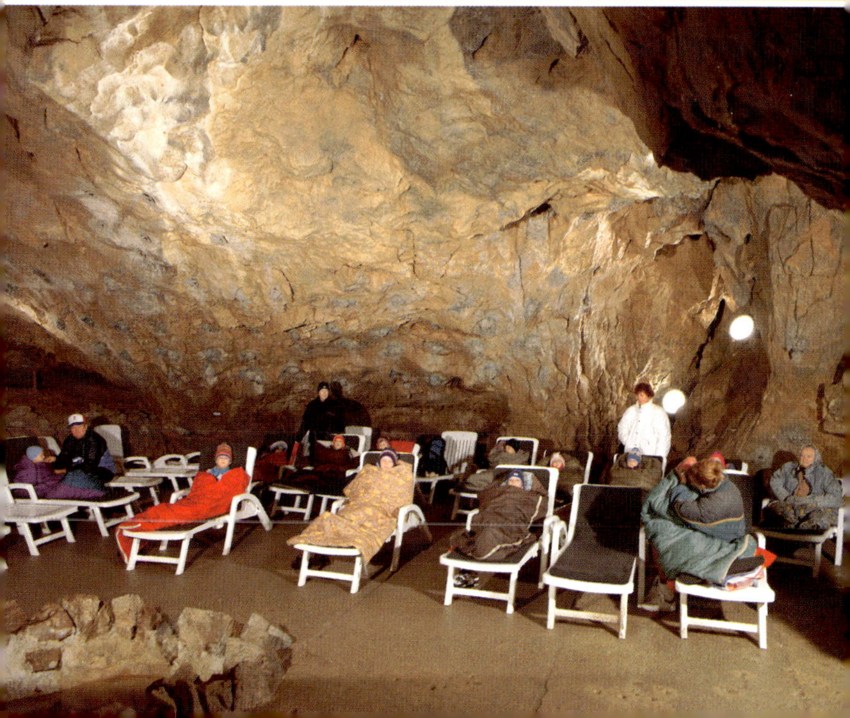

DEMÄNOVSKÁ JASKYŇA SLOBODY

NATIONAL NATURE MONUMENT
NATIONALES NATURDENKMAL

*Cadastral area/
Katastergebiet:*
Demänovská Dolina
District/Kreis:
Liptovský Mikuláš
Region/Bezirk:
Žilina

THE DEMÄNOVSKÁ CAVE OF LIBERTY

Situated on the right-hand slopes of the Demänovská Valley in the northern part of the Low Tatras National Park. Entrance to the cave is in Točište Valley, 870 m a.s.l.

It was formed in the Middle Triassic Gutenstein limestones of the Krížňanský nappe by the former underground flow of Demänovka and its lateral hanging ponor tributaries.

The cave - an integral part of an extensive cave system of the Demänovská Valley - consists of four developmental levels into which steeply descending lateral passages infall in hanging position.

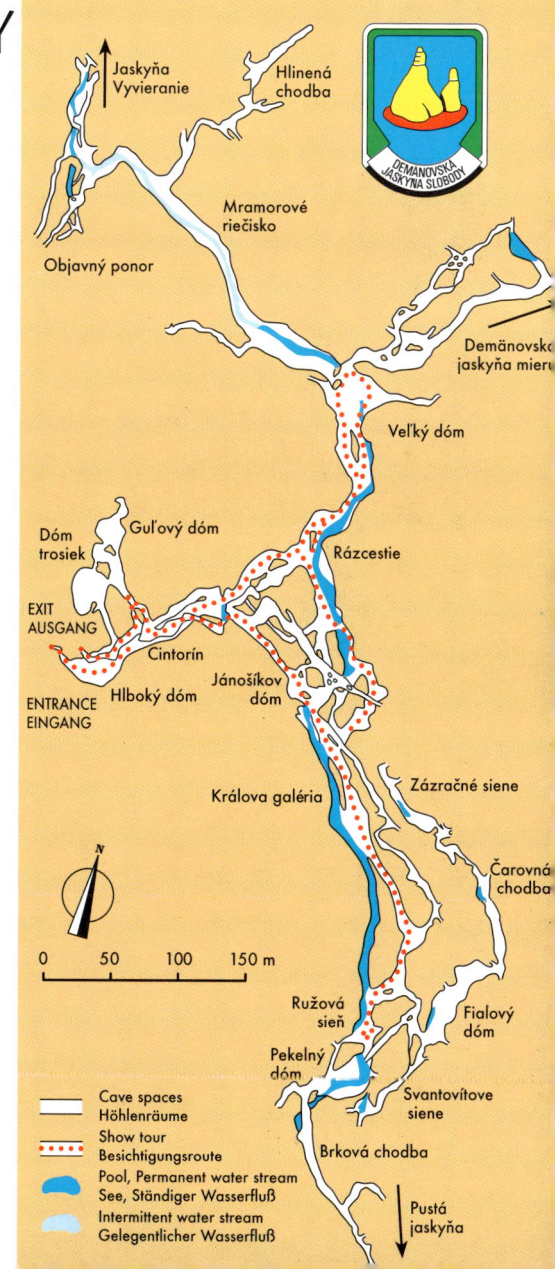

The overall length of the Demänovská Cave of Liberty exceeds more than 8,400 m.

Sinter „water-lilies" and other sinter pool formations, as well as eccentric stalactites are unique among phenomena of sinter filling. Mighty sinter waterfalls and stalagnates, sphaerolithic stalactites and many other diverse forms of stalactites and stalagmites are captivating.

An underground flow of Demänovka is running through the cave. It springs under the main crest of the Low Tatras in a non-karst area and sinks at Lúčky. The flow emerges in the cave Vyvieranie northerly to the Demänovská Cave of Liberty.

Bones of the cave bear (*Ursus spelaeus*) were found in the Medvedia corridor. Untill now 4 species of bats, have been found here *Myotis myotis* and *Rhinolophus hipposideros*.

The first man who penetrated to the cave was A. Král assisted by A. Mišura and other spelunkers in 1921. These explorations have influenced considerably further speleological explorations in Slovakia. A part of the cave was made accessible to the public in 1924, and its upper parts in 1931-1933.

The cave was interconnected to the Pustá cave in 1951. A connection with the cave Vyvieranie was reached by a speleo-diving survey in 1983. After several unsuccessful attempts, a natural connection with the Demänovská Cave of Peace was achieved at the turn of 1986 and 1987.

Since 1993, the cave serves for speleotherapeutical procedures. The present overall length of the show cave is 1,800 m. It is the most visited Slovak show cave and belongs to the most beautiful caves in Europe.

DIE FREIHEITSHÖHLE DEMÄNOVSKÁ

Die Höhle befindet sich auf der rechten Seite des Tales Demänovská dolina auf dem Nordabhang der Niederen Tatra, in der Nationalen Naturreservation Demänovská Tal im Nationalpark Niedere Tatra. Der Eingang in die Höhle ist in dem kleinen Tal Točište in 870 m ü. d. M.

Sie ist in mitteltriassischen Gutenstein-Kalksteinen der Krížna-Decke die tektonischen Störungen durch den ehemaligen unterirdischen Strom des kleinen Flusses Demänovka und seine seitlichen unterirdischen Zuflüsse entlang gebildet worden. Sie besteht aus vier Entwicklungsetagen, in welche in hängender Position vier steil sinkende Seitengänge münden. Die Höhle gehört zu dem Demänová-Höhlensystem und ist über 8400 m lang.

Von der reichen Sinterausfüllung sind sehr einzigartig die Sinterseerosen und andere Seeformen sowie exzentrische Stalaktiten. Interessant sind auch die massiven Sinterwasserfälle und Stalagnaten, sphärolithische Stalaktiten und viele andere Formen von Stalaktiten und Stalagmiten.

Durch die Höhle fließt der unterirdische Strom des Flusses Demänovka, der im Nicht-Karstgebiet unter dem Hauptkamm der Niederen Tatra quillt und in Lúčky in das Unterirdische sinkt. Auf die Oberfläche kommt er durch die Höhle Vyvieranie nördlich der Demänovská jaskyňa slobody.

In Medvedia chodba (Bärengang) wurden Knochen des Höhlenbären (*Ursus spelaeus*) gefunden. Bisher wurden vier Fledermausarten festgestellt, in den letzten Jahren Fledermaus Großmausohr (*Myotis myotis*) und Kleinhufeisennase (*Rhinolophus hipposideros*).

Im 1921 wurde diese Höhle von A. Král, A. Mišura und ihren Helfern erschlossen. Die Entdeckung dieser Höhle beeinflusste wesentlich die weitere speläologische Untersuchung in der Slowakei. Ein Teil der Höhle wurde 1924 für die Öffentlichkeit zugänglich gemacht. Die oberen Teile wurden 1931 - 1933 zugänglich gemacht.

Im Jahre 1951 wurde diese Höhle mit der Höhle Pustá jaskyňa verbunden. 1983 wurde durch Speläo-Tauchen die Verbindung mit der Höhle Vyvieranie erreicht. Nach mehreren mißerfolgreichen Versuchen wurde an der Jahreswende 1986 und 1987 die natürliche Verbindung mit der Höhle Demänovská jaskyňa mieru (Höhle des Friedens) erreicht.

Seit 1993 werden hier speläoklimatische Kuren gemacht. Der für die Öffentlichkeit zugängliche Teil ist 1800 m lang. Es ist die meist besuchte Schauhöhle der Slowakei und gehört zu den schönsten in Europa.

DEMÄNOVSKÁ ĽADOVÁ JASKYŇA

NATIONAL NATURE MONUMENT
NATIONALES NATURDENKMAL

Cadastral area/Katastergebiet: Demänovská Dolina
District/Kreis: Liptovský Mikuláš
Region/Bezirk: Žilina

THE DEMÄNOVSKÁ ICE CAVE

Situated on the right-hand slopes of the Demänovská Valley in the northern part of the Low Tatras National Park. Entrance to the cave is in the cliff called Bašta (Bastion), 840 m a.s.l.

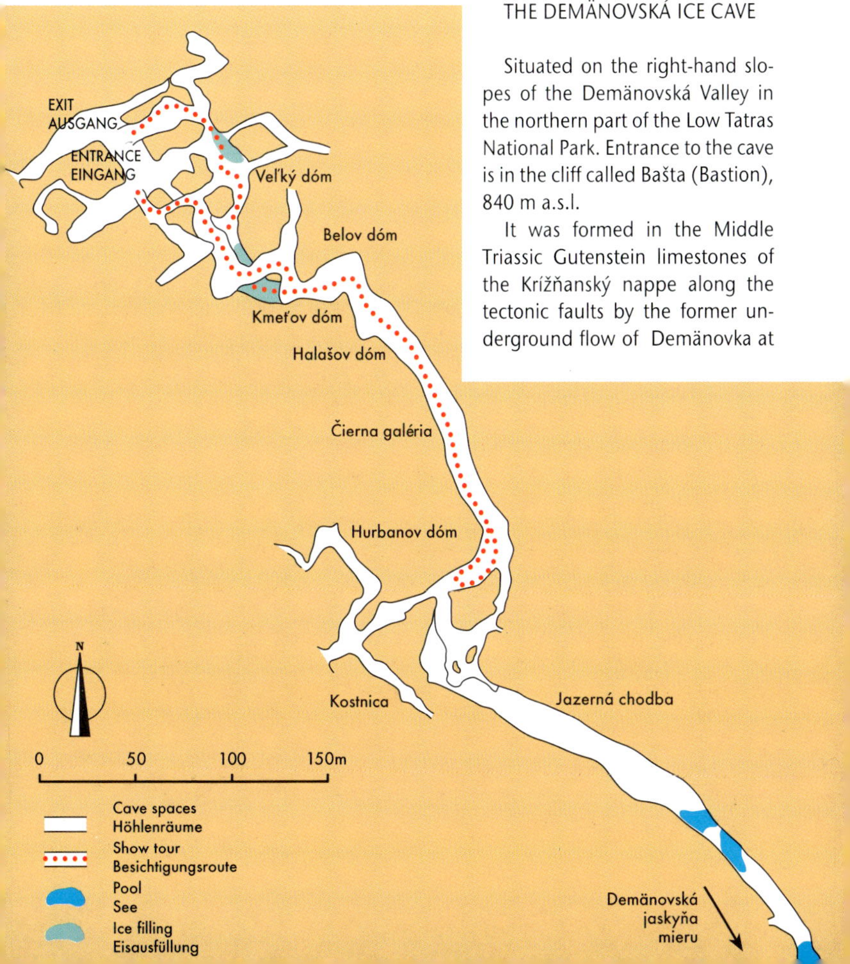

It was formed in the Middle Triassic Gutenstein limestones of the Krížňanský nappe along the tectonic faults by the former underground flow of Demänovka at three developmental levels. It represents the former spring part of the Demänová Cave System. The cave is 1,750 m long.

Ice filling occurs in the lower parts of the cave falling from the entrance down to the depth 40 - 50 m. Ground ice, ice columns, stalactites and stalagmites are present.

A long known finding place of bones of various vertebrates including cave bear (*Ursus spelaeus*) that were erroneously taken for dragon bones in the 18th century.

The cave has been known since the time immemorial. First written mention is in the Esztergom Chapter bill from 1229. It was surveyed by J. Buchholz Jr in 1714 - 1724. Numerous inscriptions on its walls (the oldest from 1714) and a lot of preserved rich literary resources from the 18th century are evidence of a great interest of the contemporary scientists and the general public.

The cave was open to the public in the eighties of the last century, and reopened in 1950 - 1952. Currently, publicly accessible are 650 m.

DIE EISHÖHLE DEMÄNOVSKÁ

Die Eishöhle befindet sich auf der rechten Seite des Demänová-Tales auf dem Nordabhang der Niederen Tatra. Sie liegt in der Nationalen Naturreservation Demänovská Tal im Nationalpark Niedere Tatra. Der Eingang in die Höhle in der Klippe Bašta liegt 840 m ü. d. M.

Sie ist in mitteltriassischen Gutenstein-Kalksteinen der Krížna-Decke die tektonischen Störungen durch den ehemaligen unterirdischen Strom des kleinen Flusses Demänovka entlang in drei Entwicklungsetagen gebildet worden. Sie stellt den ehemaligen Karstquellenteil des Demänová-Höhlensystems dar. Die Höhle ist 1750 m lang.

Die Eisausfüllung kommt in den unteren Etagen der Höhle vor. Von dem Eingang sinken sie in die Tiefe von 40 bis 50 m. Vertreten sind Bodeneis, Eissäulen, Stalaktiten und Stalagmiten.

Seit langem bekannter Fundort von Knochen verschiedener Wirbeltiere einschließlich der des Höhlenbären (*Ursus spelaeus*), die in der ersten Hälfte des 18. Jahrhunderts für Drachenknochen gehalten wurden.

Die Höhle ist seit jeher bekannt. Die erste schriftliche Erwähnung ist in der Urkunde der Ostrihomer Kapitel aus dem Jahre 1229. 1714 - 1724 wurde sie von J. Buchholtz jr. untersucht. Eine Menge Wandaufschriften (die älteste von 1714) und die erhaltene reichliche Literatur aus dem 18. Jahrhundert zeugen vom großen Interesse damaliger wissenschaftlicher Kreise sowie der Öffentlichkeit für die Höhle.

Die Höhle wurde in den 80. Jahren vorigen Jahrhunderts für die Öffentlichkeit zugänglich gemacht. Erneut wurde sie 1950 - 1952 zugänglich gemacht und heute können 650 m besichtigt werden.

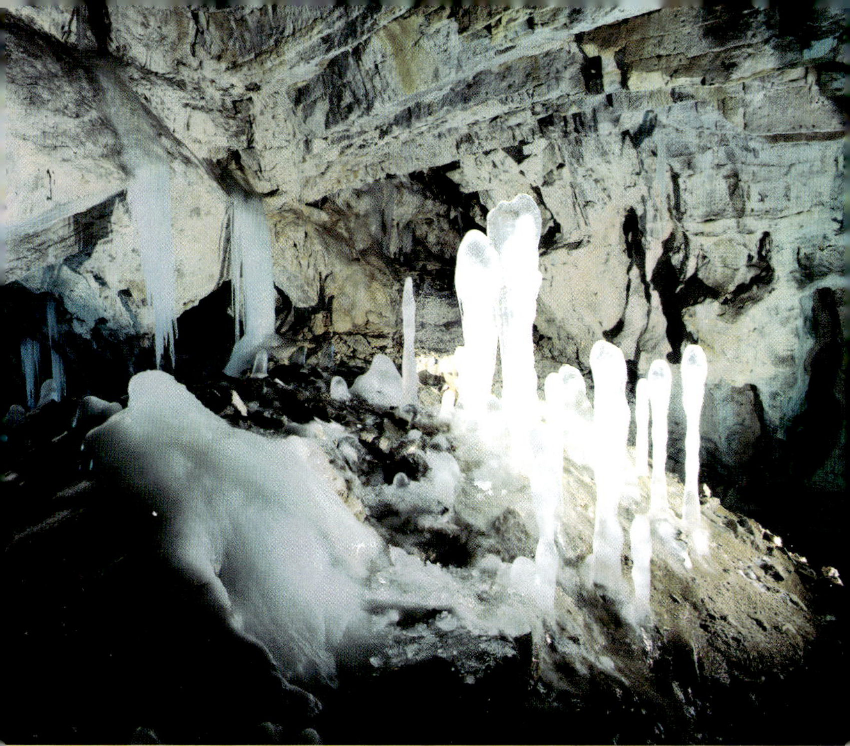

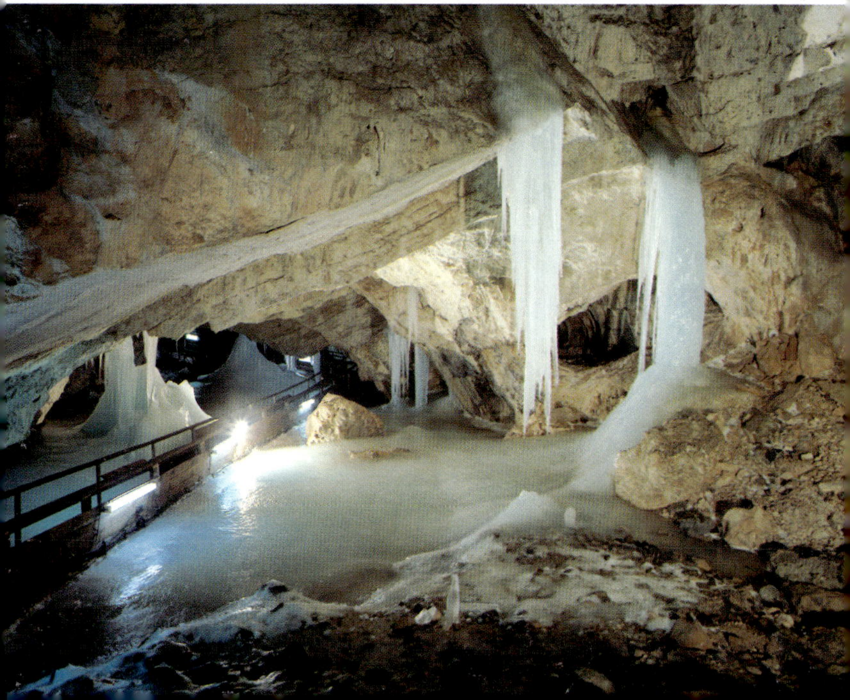

DOBŠINSKÁ ĽADOVÁ JASKYŇA

NATIONAL NATURE MONUMENT
NATIONALES NATURDENKMAL

Cadastral area/Katastergebiet: Dobšiná
District/Kreis: Rožňava
Region/Bezirk: Košice

THE DOBŠINSKÁ ICE CAVE

It is situated in the Slovak Paradise in the Spiš-Gemer Karst in the National Nature Reserve Stratená within the territory of the Slovak Paradise National Park. Entrance to the cave is on the northern slope of Duča hill, 971 m a.s.l.

It was formed in the Middle Triassic Steinalm and Wetterstein limestones of the Silický nappe along the tectonic faults and interbed surfaces, by the former underground stream of Hnilec river at three developmental levels. It belongs to the genetic system of the Stratenská Cave. The cave length is 1,232 m and vertical range is 112 m.

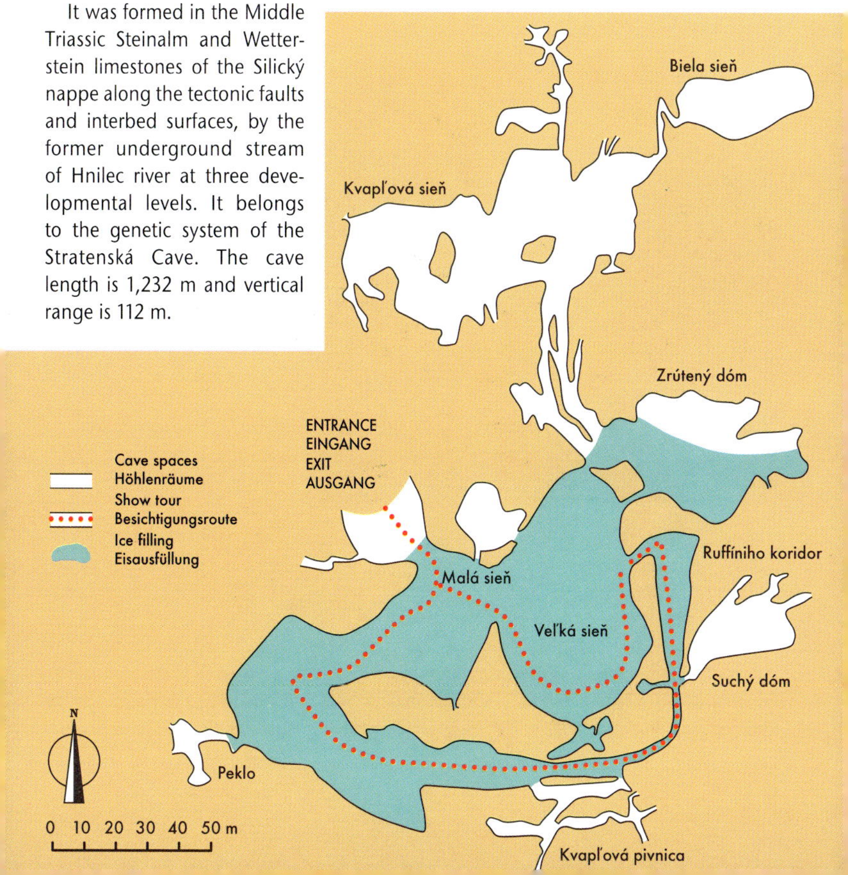

Cave spaces / Höhlenräume
Show tour / Besichtigungsroute
Ice filling / Eisausfüllung

0 10 20 30 40 50 m

Ice filling occurs in the form of ground ice, ice „waterfalls", ice stalagmites and columns. The ice-covered area is 9,772 sq. m, and the total volume of ice is 110,132 cubic meters. The maximum thickness of ice is in the Great Hall 26.5 m. It ranks among the most important ice caves in the world thanks to its character of glaciation. The cave is one of the most important winter refuges of bats - *Myotis mystacinus* and *Myotis brandti* in Slovakia.

The cave was discovered in 1870 by E. Ruffíni assisted by G. Lang, A. Mega, and F. Fehér. It was open to the public as early as in 1871. Since 1887 it has been the first cave with electric illumination in that-time Hungary. Along with Postojna Cave it ranks among the first electrically illuminated caves in Europe. Currently, 475 m of the cave are open to the public.

DIE EISHÖHLE DOBŠINSKÁ

Die Eishöhle liegt in Slovenský raj (Slowakisches Paradies) im Karstgebiet Spišsko-gemerský kras. Sie liegt in der Nationalen Naturreservation Stratená im Nationalpark Slovenský raj.

Der Eingang in die Höhle auf dem Nordabhang des Berges Duča liegt 971 m ü.d.M.

Die Höhle ist in den mitteltriassischen Steinalm- und Wetterstein-Kalksteinen der Silica-Decke die tektonischen Störungen und Schichtenzwischenflächen durch den ehemaligen unterirdischen Strom des Flusses Hnilec entlang in drei Entwicklungsetagen gebildet worden. Ihre Länge beträgt 1232 m, die vertikale Spannweite ist 112 m. Die Eisausfüllung kommt in Form von Bodeneis, Eisfällen, Eisstalagmiten und Säulen vor. Die Eisfläche beträgt 9772 m^2, das Eisvolumen ist 110 132 m^3. Die größte Dicke der Eisschicht ist im Großen Saal und beträgt 26,5 m. Mit ihrem Charakter der Vereisung gehört sie zu den bedeutsamsten Eishöhlen der Welt. Eine der wichtigsten Winterquartiere von *Myotis mystacinus* und *Myotis brandti* in der Slowakei.

Die Höhle wurde von E. Ruffíni, G. Lang, A. Mega und F. Fehér im Jahre 1870 entdeckt. Bereits 1871 wurde sie zugänglich gemacht. Seit 1887 war es die erste elektrisch beleuchtete Höhle im damaligen Ungarn. Gemeinsam mit der Höhle Postojnska gehört sie zu den ersten elektrisch beleuchteten Höhlen in Europa. Derzeit sind 475 m zugänglich.

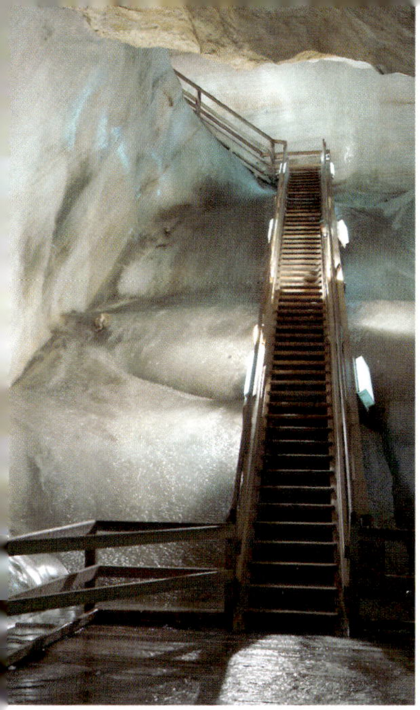
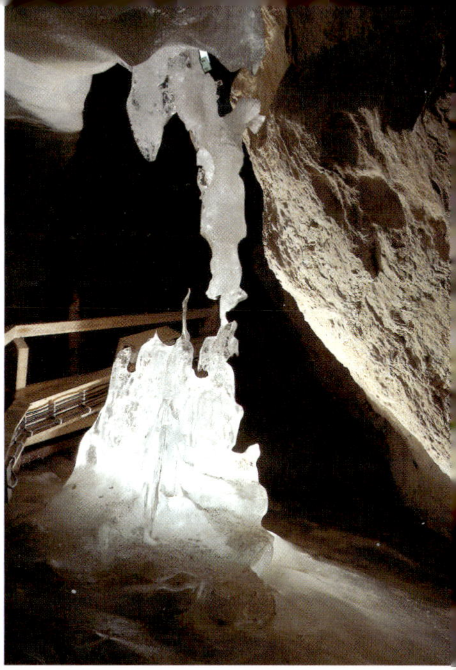
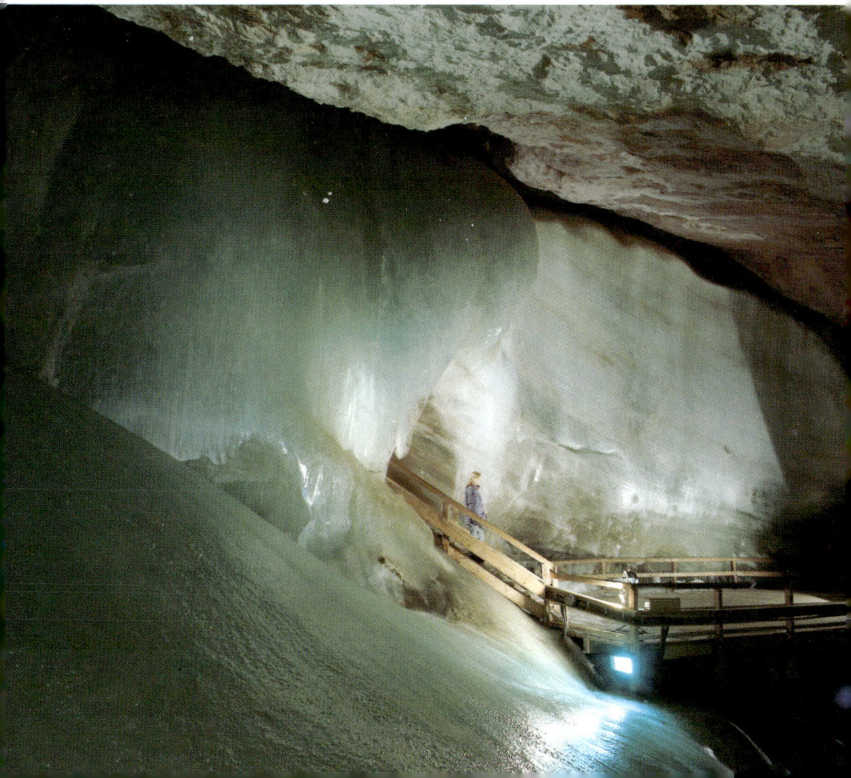

DOMICA

NATIONAL NATURE MONUMENT
WORLD NATURAL HERITAGE
NATIONALES NATURDENKMAL
WELTNATURERBE

*Cadastral area/
Katastergebiet:* Kečovo
District/Kreis: Rožňava
Region/Bezirk: Košice

THE DOMICA CAVE

It is situated on the southwestern edge of the Silická Plateau in the Slovak Karst, 10 km to the southwest of Plešivec, near the borders with Hungary. Domica Cave is a pearl of the National Nature Reserve Domické škrapy (Domické Karren) in the Protected Landscape Area and Biospherical Reserve of the Slovak Karst. Entrance to the cave is at the southern foothill of Domica Hill, 339 m a.s.l.

It was formed in the Middle Triassic Wetterstein limestones of the Silický nappe along the tectonic faults, by underground streams of Styx and Domica at three developmental levels. Overall cave length is 5,080 m. The lowest part is filled with gravel and loam. It forms a genetically compact entity, about 25 km in length, together with the Baradla Cave in Hungary.

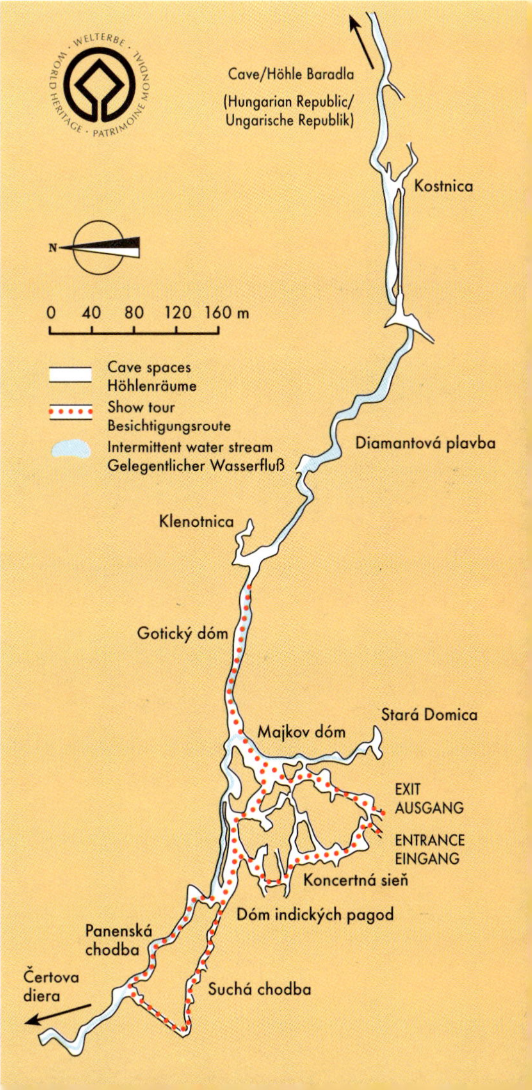

Shields and drums, cascading pools, onion-shaped stalactites and pagoda-like stalagmites are typical for its rich sinter filling.

Bones of spelean bear (*Ursus spelaeus*) were excavated in the Suchá corridor. Among 11 species of the known bats prevails *Rhinolophus euryale*, forming here a unique colony in Slovakia (more than 1,000 bats).

It is the most important finding-place of the Neolithic „bukovohorská" culture (4,000 years B.C.). Pile holes of dwellings and fire places have been preserved in this cave. Abundance of shatters give evidence of ceramics manufacture. Assorted findings represent the top of the Neolithic handling of bones. Even the evidence of cloths production have been found. The rear parts of the cave had probably been ritual places, what is to be seen by carbon drawings. Findings of artifacts with eastern lineary ornamented pottery and items from the Early Stone Age - Szeletien - from 35,000 years ago are unique as well.

The Old Domica Cave has been known long. Its continuation into the new spaces was discovered by J. Majko in 1926. Domica Cave was interconnected to the cave Čertova diera in 1929 and to the cave Baradla in 1932.

It was made accessible to the public in 1932, including an underground boat trip. Catastrophic floods flooded the cave in June, 1954. Other floods were in 1955, 1964, 1977 and 1981. Currently, the show cave tour is 1,315 m, including a 140 m boat trip.

DIE HÖHLE DOMICA

Die Höhle befindet sich am südwestlichen Rand des Plateaus Silická planina in Slovenský kras, 10 km südöstlich von Plešivec in der Nähe von der Staatsgrenze zu der Ungarischen Republik. Sie liegt in der Nationalen Naturreservation Domické škrapy auf dem Gebiet des Landschaftsschutzgebietes Biosphärische Reservation Slowakischer Karst. Der Eingang in die Höhle auf dem Südabhang des gleichnamigen Berges liegt 339 m ü. d. M.

Sie ist in mitteltriassischen Wetterstein-Kalksteinen der Silica-Decke die tektonischen Störungen durch unterirdische Ströme der Bäche Styx und Domica entlang in drei Entwicklungsetagen gebildet worden. Die Länge der Höhle beträgt 5080 m. Die niedrigste Etage ist mit Schotter und Ton verschlämmt. Sie bildet eine genetische Einheit mit der Höhle Baradla in Ungarn mit Gesamtlänge von ca. 25 km.

Aus der reichen Sinterausfüllung sind Schilder und Trommel, Kaskadenseen, zwiebelförmige Stalaktiten und pagodenförmige Stalagmiten typisch.

Im Gang Suchá chodba wurden Knochen des Höhlenbären (*Ursus spelaeus*) gefunden. Von den bisher festgestellten Fledermausarten ist die Mittelmeer-Hufeisennase (*Rhinolophus euryale*) dominierend, die eine Kolonie von ca. 1000 Fledermausen bildet, einzige dieser Art auf dem Gebiet der Slowakei.

Der wichtigste Höhlenfundort der Bukovohorska-Kultur aus dem Neolithikum (4000 Jahre v. u. Z.). In der Höhle sind Kreisgruben von Wohnobjekten und Feuerstätten erhalten geblieben. Keramikherstellung wird durch viele Scherben von Tongefäßen nachgewiesen. Mehrere Entdeckungen repräsentieren die Spitze der neolithischen Knochenbearbeitung. Ebenso wurden hier auch Beweise für Gewebeherstellung gefunden. Hintere Teile der Höhle waren wahrscheinlich Kultstätten, was die Kohleaufzeichnungen andeuten. Einmalig sind die Entdeckungen einer Kultur mit östlicher linealischer Keramik und 35 000 Jahre alte Entdeckungen (Szeletien) aus der älteren Steinzeit.

Die alte Domica-Höhle war vor sehr langer Zeit bekannt. Die Fortsetzung der Höhlenräume wurde 1926 von J. Majko entdeckt. Domica wurde 1929 mit der Höhle Čertova diera verbunden, mit der Höhle Baradla 1932. Seit 1932 zugänglich, einschließlich der unterirdischen Bootfahrt.

Im Juni 1954 wurde die Höhle vom katastrophischen Hochwasser betroffen. Weitere Überschwemmungen folgten in 1955, 1964, 1977 und 1981.

Die derzeit betriebenen zugänglichen Teile sind 1315 m lang, die Bootfahrt ist 140 m lang.

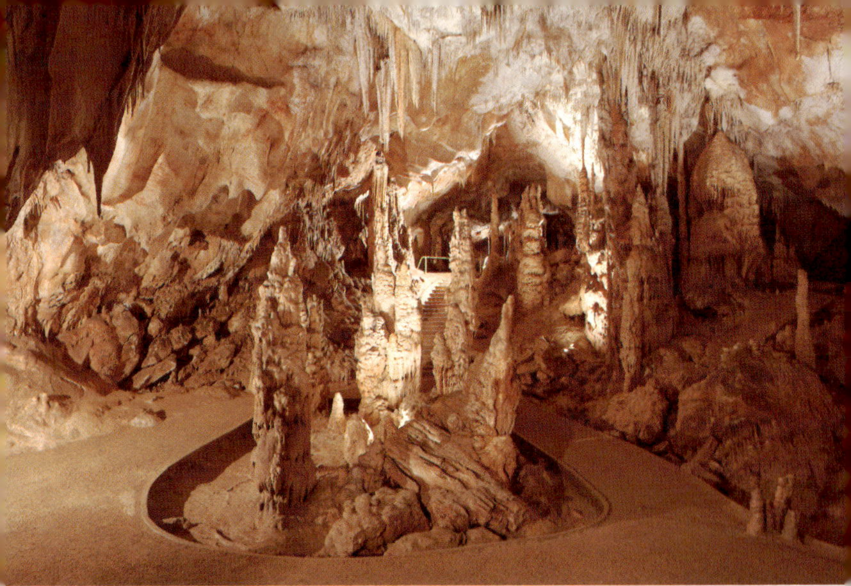

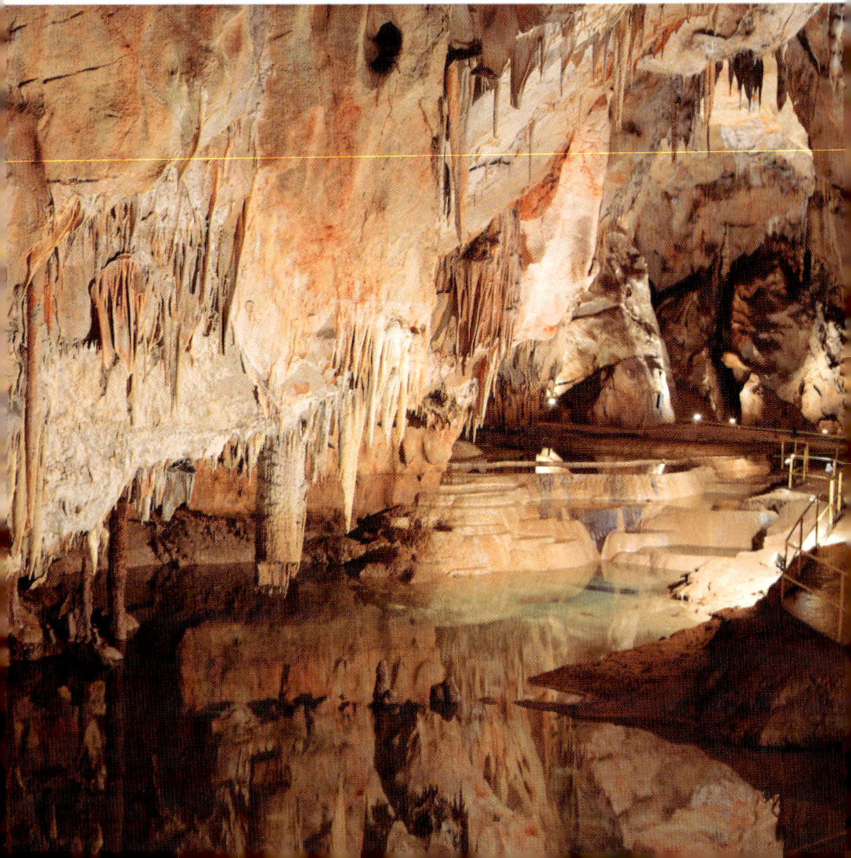

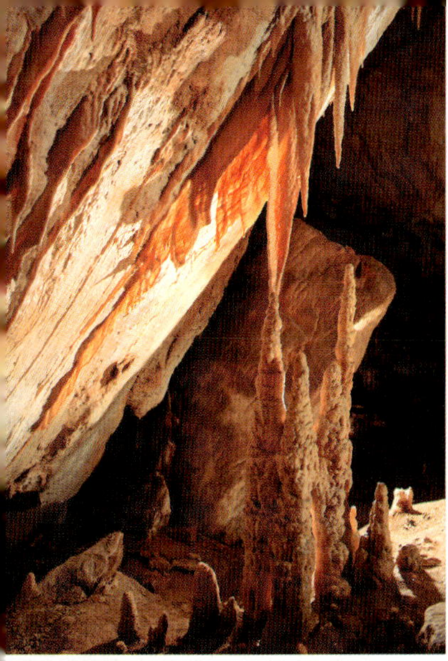
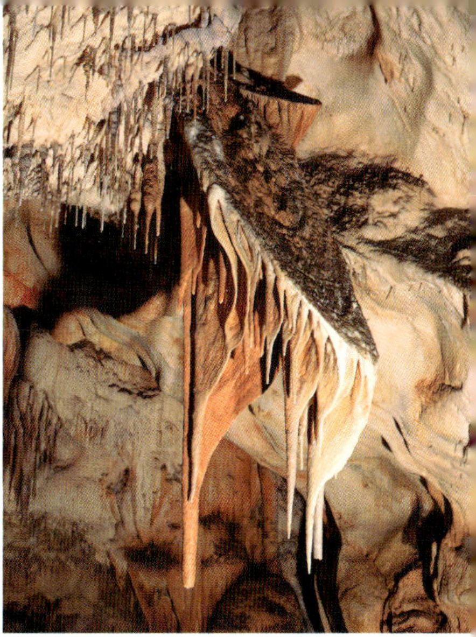
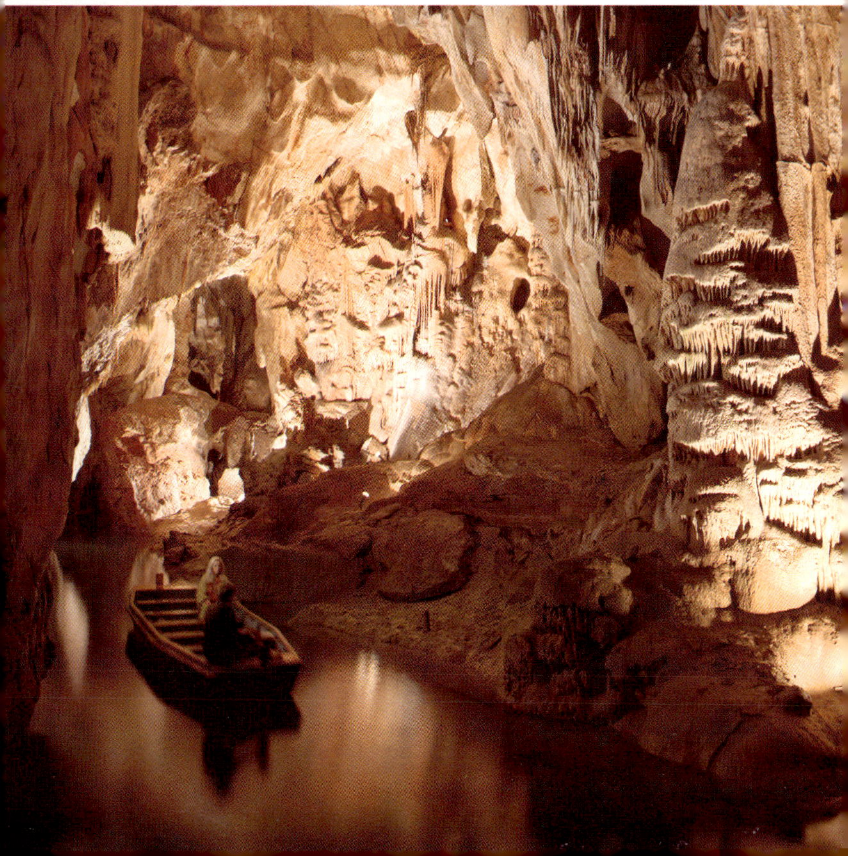

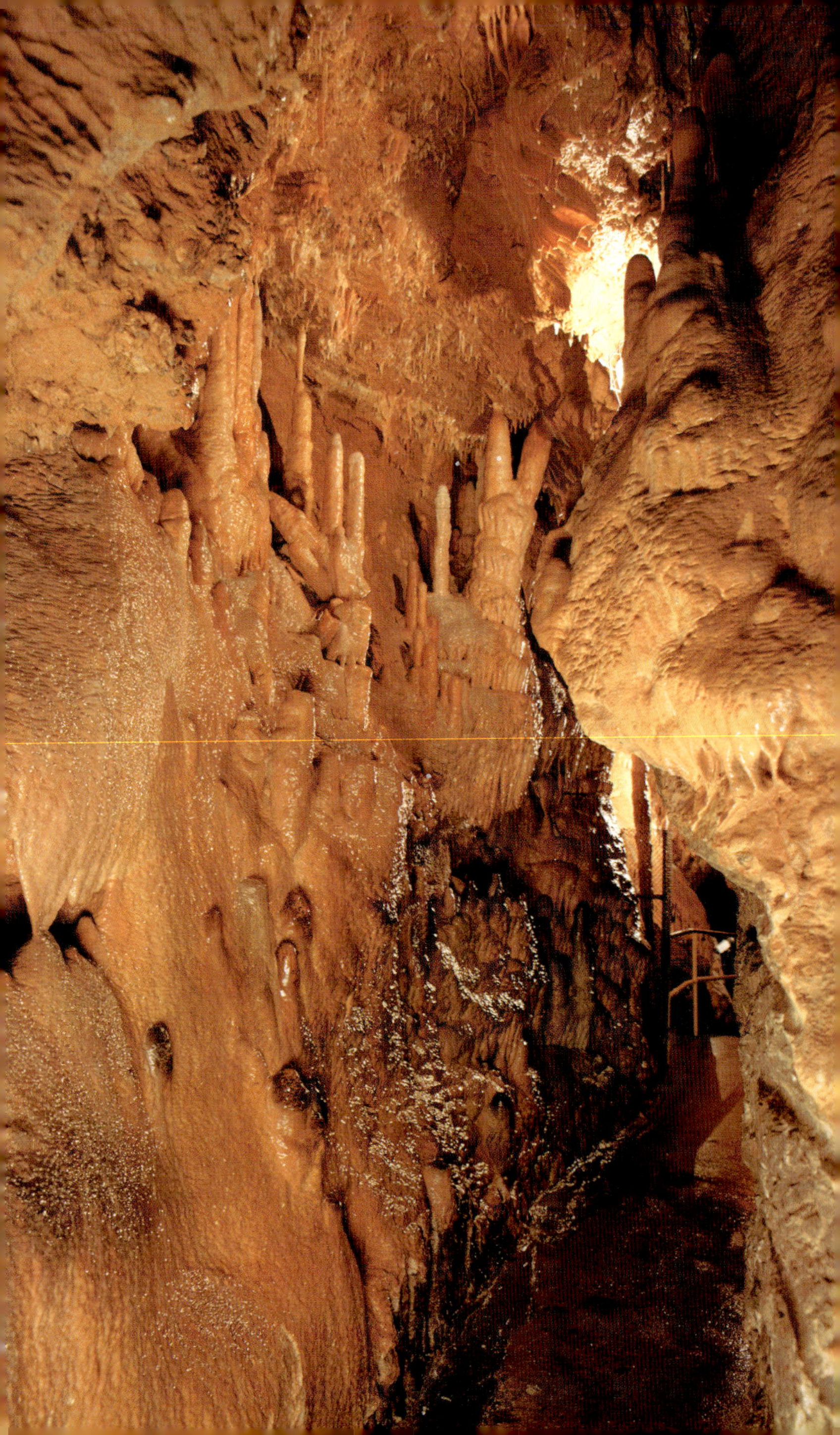

DRINY

NATIONAL NATURE MONUMENT
NATIONALES NATURDENKMAL

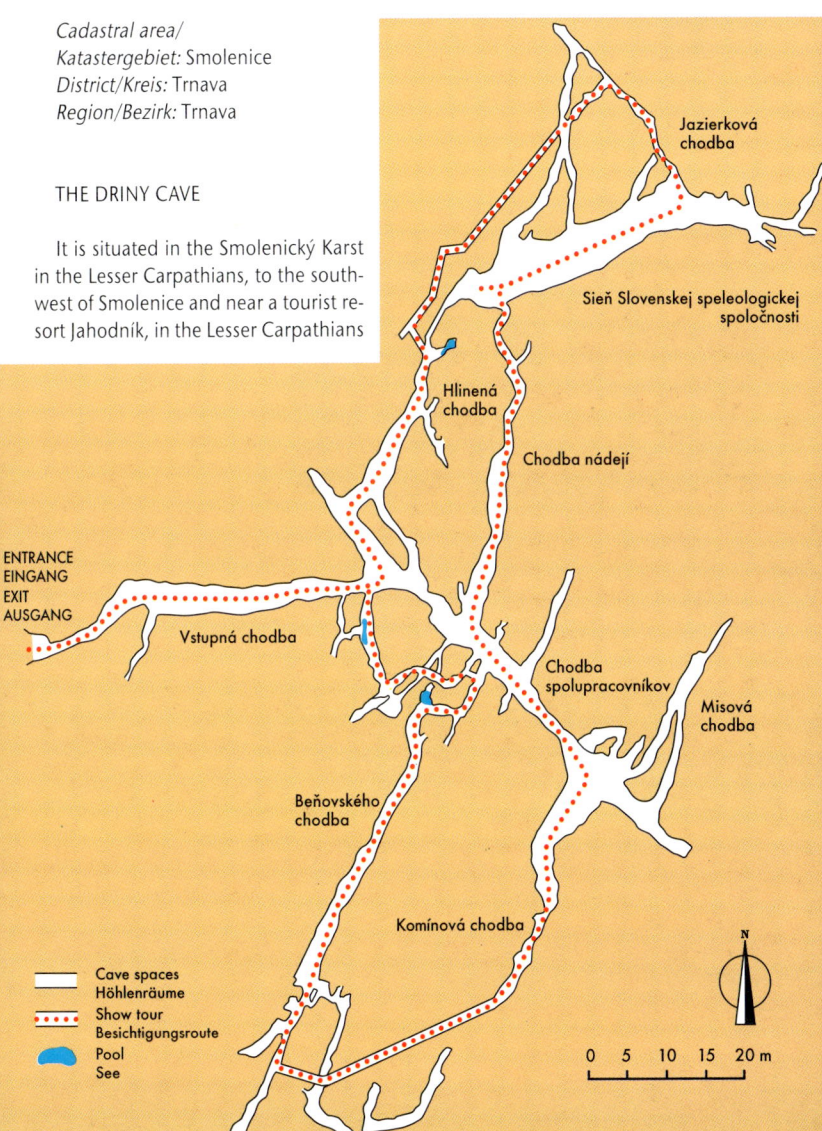

Cadastral area/
Katastergebiet: Smolenice
District/Kreis: Trnava
Region/Bezirk: Trnava

THE DRINY CAVE

It is situated in the Smolenický Karst in the Lesser Carpathians, to the southwest of Smolenice and near a tourist resort Jahodník, in the Lesser Carpathians

Jazierková chodba

Sieň Slovenskej speleologickej spoločnosti

Hlinená chodba

Chodba nádejí

ENTRANCE
EINGANG
EXIT
AUSGANG

Vstupná chodba

Chodba spolupracovníkov

Misová chodba

Beňovského chodba

Komínová chodba

Cave spaces / Höhlenräume
Show tour / Besichtigungsroute
Pool / See

0 5 10 15 20 m

Protected Landscape Area. Entrance to the cave is on the southwestern slope of Cejtach Hill, 399 m a.s.l.

It was formed in the Lower Cretaceous marl limestones of the Vysocká series of the Krížňanský nappe by the corrosion of precipitation waters along the tectonic faults. It reaches the length of 680 m.

Less extensive cave spaces are richly decorated with sinter fillings. Draperies with tooth-like edging, sinter waterfalls, onflows, pagoda-like stalagmites, stalactites and sinter pools are typical for this cave.

The cave was discovered by J. Banič and J. Vajsábel assisted by Š. Banič, the inventor of parashute, and A. Vajsábel in 1929. It was open to the public in 1935 by the lower thirled entrance. The rear parts of the cave have been open to visitors since 1959. The show route was circulated by thirling of several connection galleries. Current show tour is 410 m long.

DIE HÖHLE DRINY

Die Höhle befindet sich im Smolenice-Karstgebiet in den Kleinen Karpaten südwestlich von Smolenice, in der Nähe vom Erholungszentrum Jahodník. Sie liegt auf dem Gebiet des Landschaftsschutzgebietes Kleine Karpaten. Der Eingang in die Höhle auf dem südwestlichen Abhang des Berges Cejtach liegt in der Höhe 399 m ü. d. M.

Sie ist in den Kalksteinen der unteren Kreide-Ära der Krížna-Decke durch Korrosion der atmosphärischen Gewässer die tektonischen Störungen entlang entstanden. Sie ist 680 m lang.

Die weniger umfangreichen Höhlenräume sind mit reichlicher Sinterausfüllung dekoriert. Typisch sind Sintervorhänge mit zahnförmigem Saum. Es gibt hier auch Wasserfälle und Aufschwemmungen, pagodenförmige Stalagmiten, Stalaktiten und kleine Seen.

Die Höhle wurde 1929 von J. Banič und J. Vajsábel mit Hilfe von Š. Banič, dem Fallschirmerfinder, und A. Vajsábel entdeckt. Für die Öffentlichkeit ist die Höhle seit 1935 durch einen unteren ausgeschachteten Eingang offen. Die hinteren Teile der Höhle sind seit 1959 zugänglich. Die Besichtigungsroute wurde durch mehrere Stollen in Kreisrundgang verbunden.

Derzeit sind 410 m zugänglich.

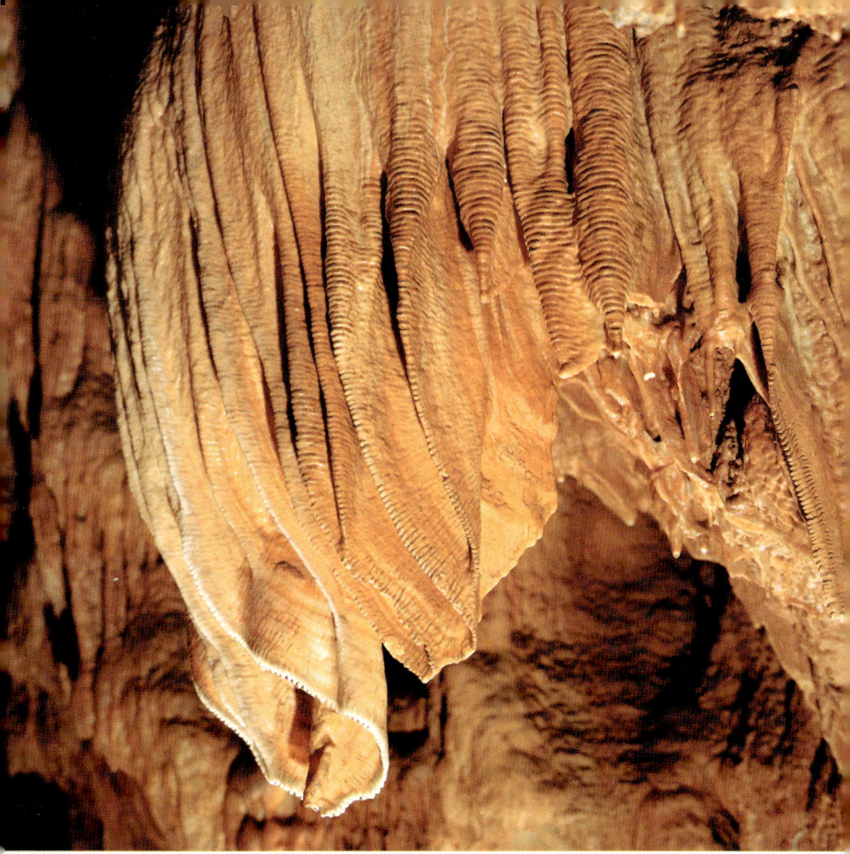
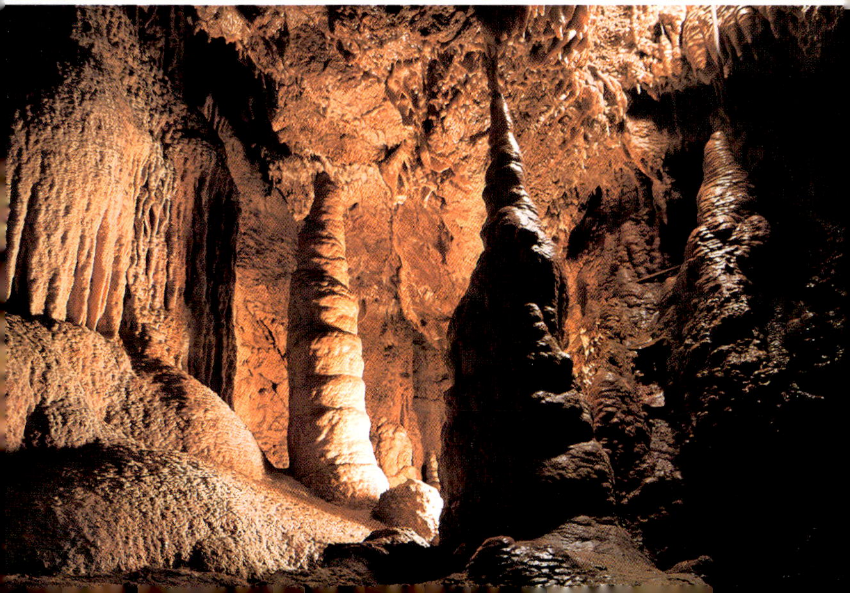

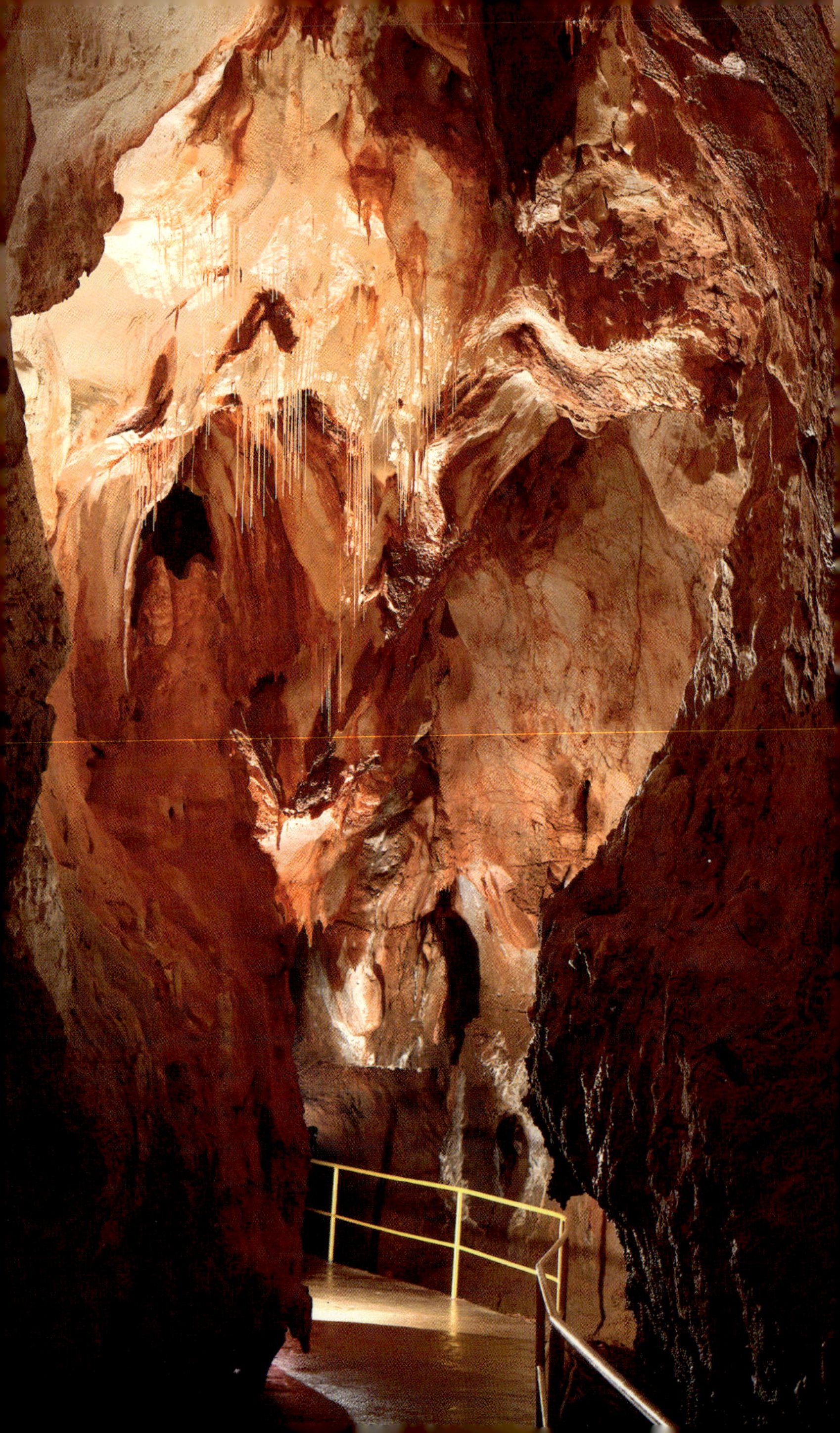

GOMBASECKÁ JASKYŇA

NATIONAL NATURE MONUMENT
WORLD NATURAL HERITAGE
NATIONALES NATURDENKMAL
WELTNATURERBE

Cadastral area/Katastergebiet: Slavec
District/Kreis: Rožňava
Region/Bezirk: Košice

THE GOMBASECKÁ CAVE

It is situated at the western foothill of the Silická Plateau, on the left bank of the canyon of Slaná river between Rožňava and Plešivec, in the Protected Landscape Area and Biospheric Reserve of the Slovak Karst. Entrance to the cave is 250 m a.s.l.

It was formed in the Middle Triassic Wetterstein limestones of the Silický nappe along tectonic faults eroded by Čierny potok (Black Brook) and its tributaries, at two developmental levels. Overall length of the seepage cave is 1,525 m.

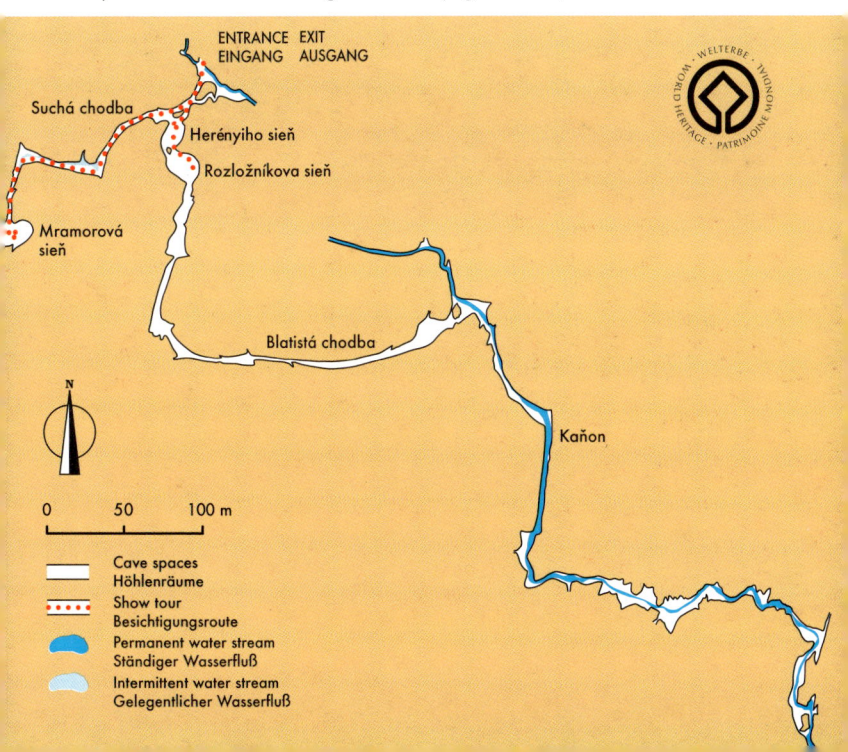

The cave was discovered in 1951 by spelunkers of Rožňava, members of the Slovak Speleological Society. It excells with its unique tiny sinter straw stalactites reaching up to 3 m. The cave is open to the public since 1955, in the length of 285 m. In 1968 it was introduced for speleotherapeutical procedures, as the first of the caves in Slovakia.

DIE HÖHLE GOMBASECKÁ

Die Höhle befindet sich im westlichen Teil des Plateaus Silická planina im Karstgebiet Slovenský kras, auf der linken Seite des Flusses Slaná zwischen den Städten Rožňava und Plešivec. Sie liegt im Landschaftsschutzgebiet der Biosphärischen Reservation Slowakische Karst. Der Eingang in die Höhle liegt 250 m ü. d. M.

Sie ist in mitteltriassischen Wetterstein-Kalksteinen der Silica-Decke die tektonischen Störungen durch den Bach Čierny Potok und seine Zuflüsse entlang in zwei Entwicklungsetagen gebildet worden. Die Länge der Karstquellenhöhle beträgt 1525 m.

Typisch sind die einzigartigen Sinterröhrchen, manchmal auch von 3 m Länge. Die Höhle wurde 1951 von den freiwilligen, in der Slowakischen Speläologie-Gesellschaft vereinigten Höhlenforschern aus Rožňava entdeckt. Seit 1955 ist sie zugänglich mit einer Länge von 285 m. Im Jahre 1968 wurde sie als die erste Höhle in der Slowakei für Speläotherapie eingesetzt.

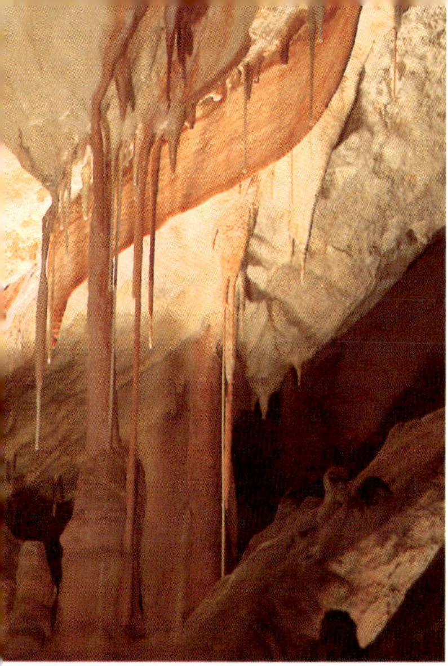
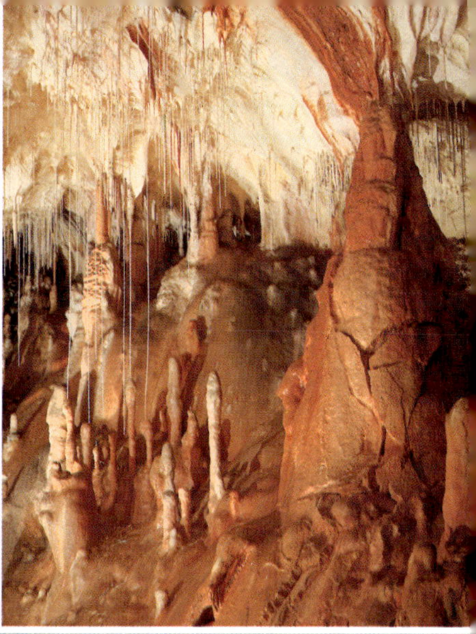
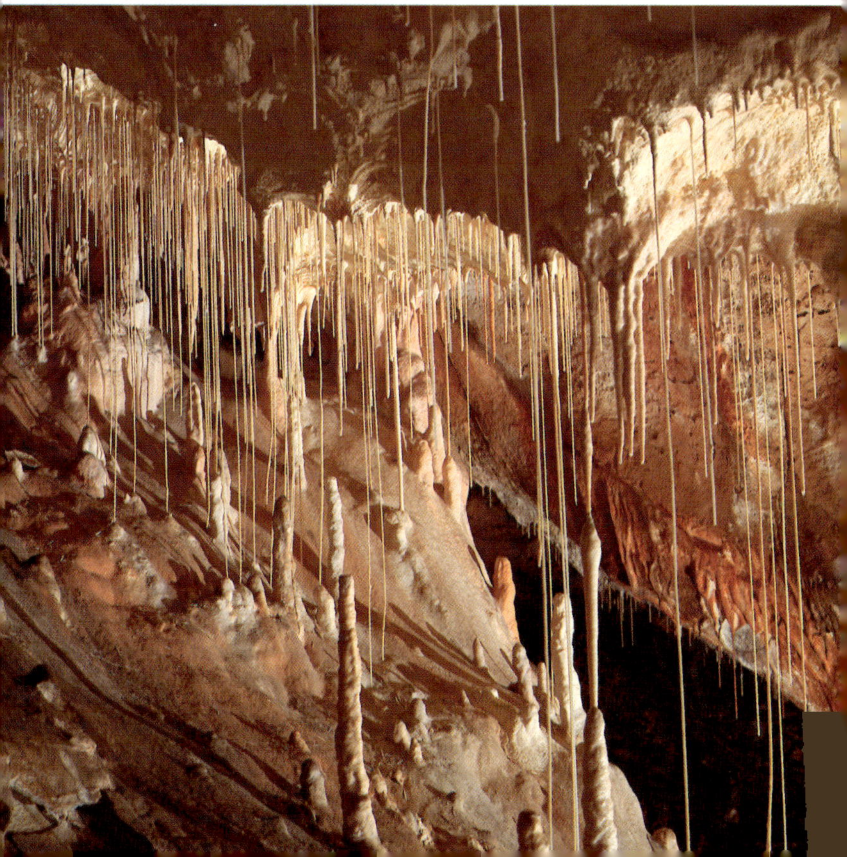

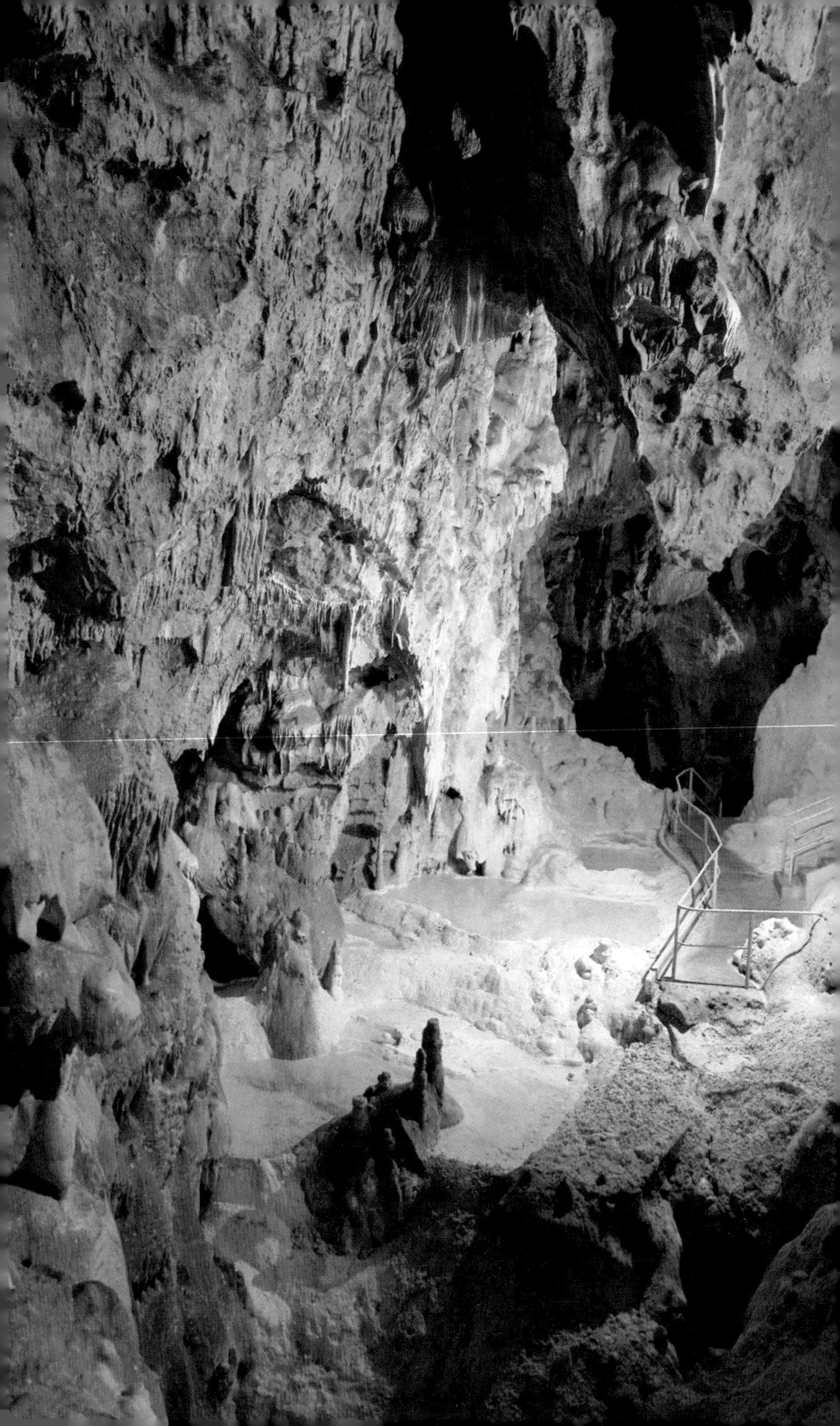

HARMANECKÁ JASKYŇA

NATIONAL NATURE MONUMENT
NATIONALES NATURDENKMAL

*Cadastral area
Katastergebiet:*
Dolný Harmanec
District/Kreis:
Banská Bystrica
Region/Bezirk:
Banská Bystrica

THE HARMANECKÁ CAVE

It is situated in the Harmanecká Valley, to the northwest of Banská Bystrica, in southern part of the Greater Fatra Protected Landscape Area, near the main road connecting Harmanec with Turčianske Teplice. Entrance to the cave is on the northern slope of Kotolnica hill, 821 m a.s.l.

It was formed in the Middle Triassic Gutenstein limestones of the Krížňanský nappe by the ancient paleoflow along the tectonic faults at two developmental levels. The overall length of the cave is about 2,500 m, at a vertical range of 75 m.

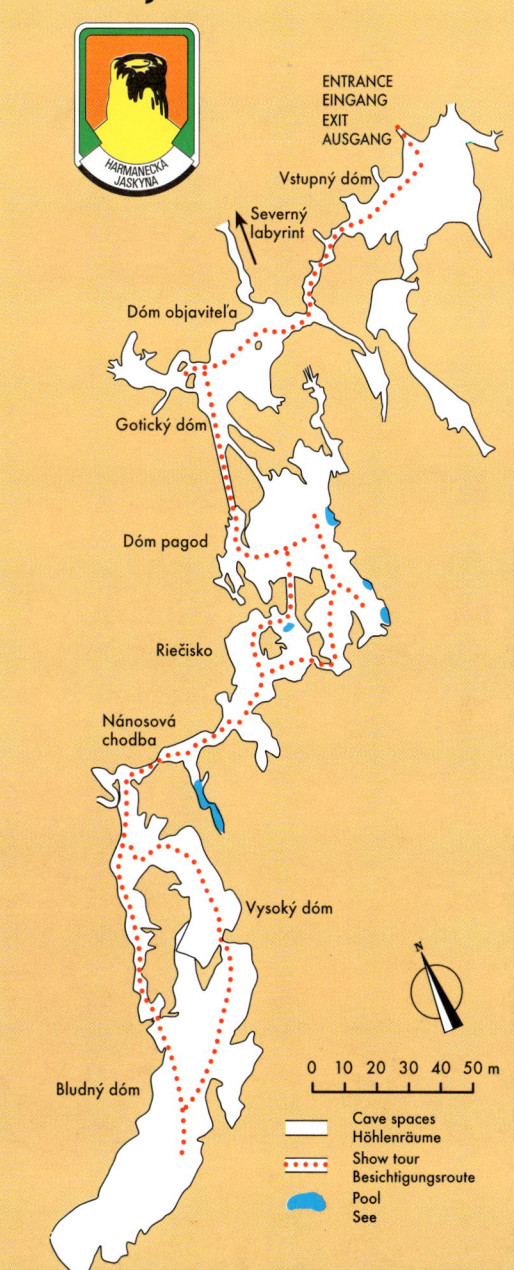

The cave is known for a rich occurrence of white soft sinter. Mighty pagoda-like stalagmites, sinter waterfalls, draperies and sinter pools can easily catch your eyes. The cave shelters 9 species of bats with the dominant *Myotis myotis* - having the colony of about 1,000 members. Its winter colony ranks among the most important ones in Slovakia.

The entrance space called Izbica (Little Chamber) has been known to the locals since the ancient times. M. Bacúrik penetrated to farther spaces in 1932. 720 m are accessible to the public since 1950.

DIE HÖHLE HARMANECKÁ

Die Höhle befindet sich im Harmanec-Tal nordwestlich von Banská Bystrica, im südlichen Teil des Gebirges Große Fatra im Landschaftsschutzgebiet Große Fatra, nicht weit von der Straßenverbindung Harmanec - Turčianske Teplice. Der Eingang in die Höhle ist auf dem nördlichen Abhang des Berges Kotolnica in einer Höhe von 821 m ü. d. M.

Sie ist in mitteltriassischen Gutenstein-Kalksteinen der Krížna-Decke durch einen alten Paläofluß die tektonischen Störungen entlang in zwei Entwicklungsetagen gebildet worden. Die Länge der Höhle beträgt ca. 2500 m bei vertikaler Spannweite von 75 m.

Die Höhle ist durch reiches Vorkommen von weißem Weichsinter bekannt. Interessant sind massive pagodenförmige Stalagmiten, Sinterwasserfälle und Vorhänge sowie kleine Sinterseen. In der Höhle leben 9 Fledermausarten. Dominant (ca. 1000 Stück) ist die Fledermaus Großmausohr (*Myotis myotis*). Ihre Winterkolonie ist eine der wichtigsten in der Slowakei.

Der Eintritt in die Höhle - genannt Izbica - war den dortigen Einwohnern seit jeher bekannt. Die weiteren Räumen wurden 1932 von M. Bacúrik entdeckt. Set 1950 sind 720 m für die Öffentlichkeit erschlossen.

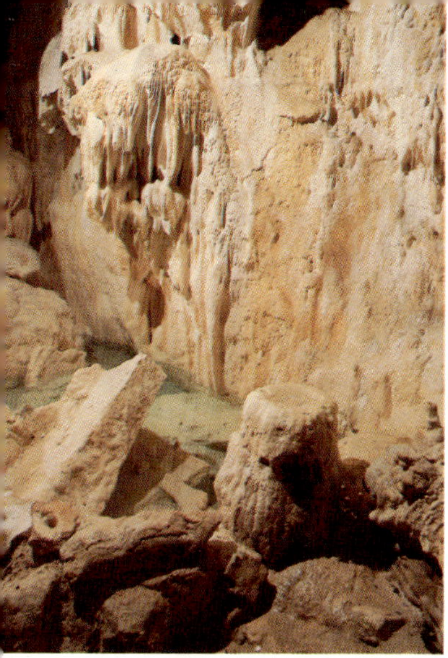

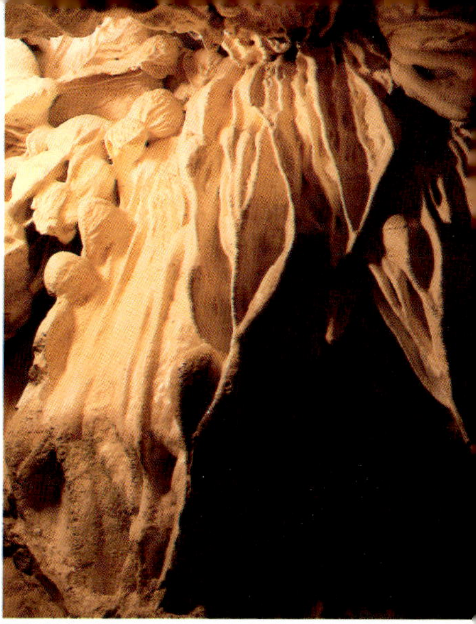

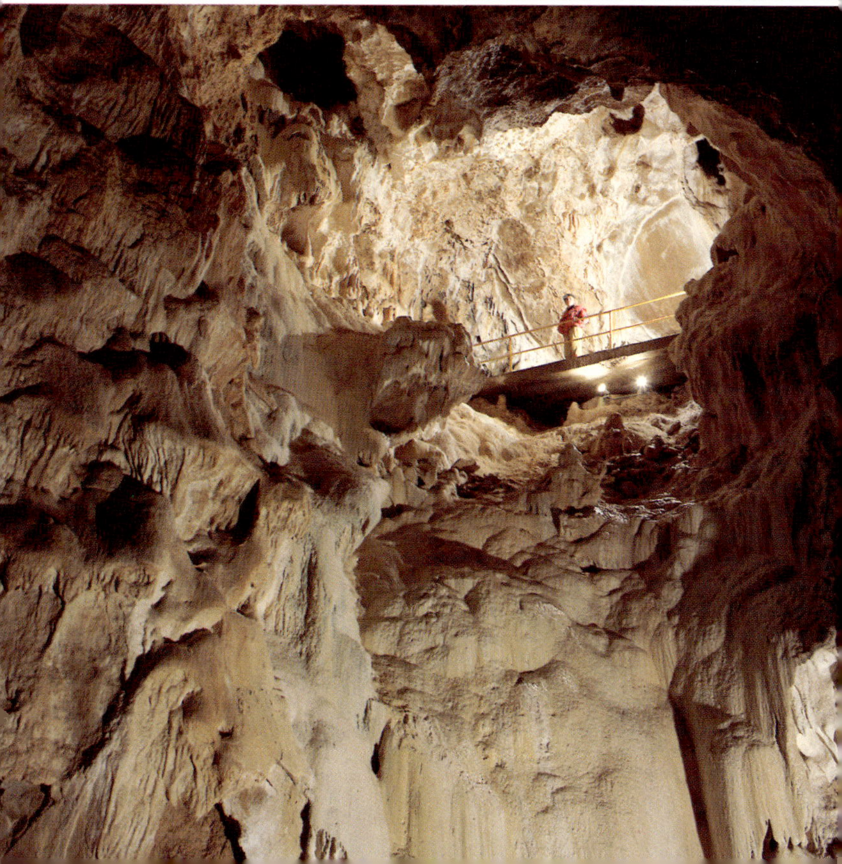

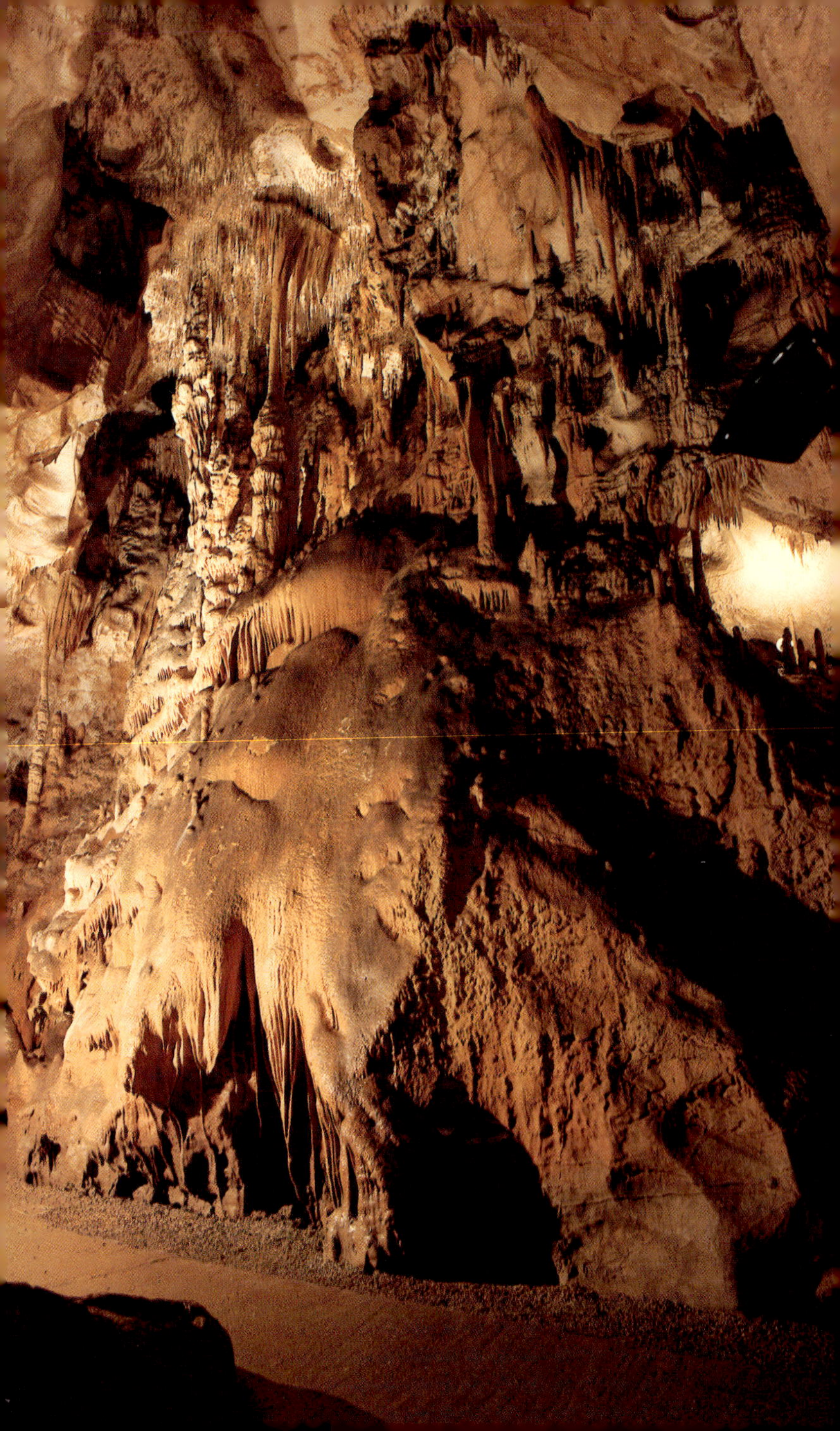

JASOVSKÁ JASKYŇA

NATIONAL NATURE MONUMENT
WORLD NATURAL HERITAGE

NATIONALES
NATURDENKMAL
WELTNATURERBE

*Cadastral area
Katastergebiet:*
Jasov
District/Kreis:
Košice-okolie
Region/Bezirk:
Košice

THE JASOVSKÁ CAVE

It is situated in the Medzevská Upland at its joint with the east margin of the Jasovská Plateau in the Slovak Karst, at the west border of Jasov. It is located in the National Nature Reserve Jasovské dubiny in the territory of the Protected Landscape Area and Biospheric Reserve of the Slovak Karst. The entrance to the cave is at the eastern foothill of Jasovská Rock, 257 m a.s.l.

It was formed in the Middle Triassic Gutenstein dolomites, Steinalm limestones and dolomites of the Silický nappe along tectonic faults, by the former underground waters of Bodva river, at five developmental levels.

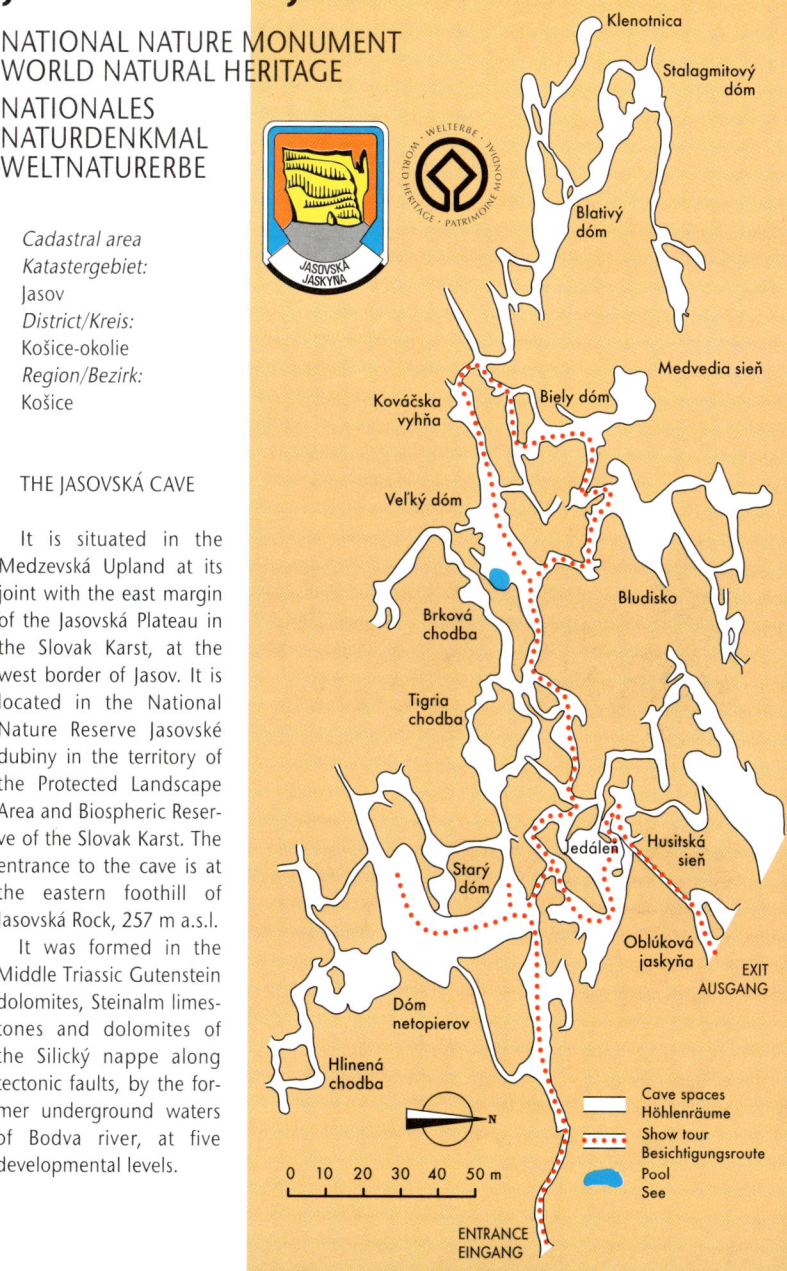

It reaches the length of 2,122 m, with vertical range 55 m.

Rich sinter filling is represented by pagoda-like stalagmites, stalagnates, shields, drums, straw stalactites and other forms.

The lowest parts of the cave are often flooded as a result of vertical movements of underground water. The lowest water level of the cave lake is 7 m below the surface flow of Bodva, the waters of which are not flowing through the cave at present.

Bones of cave bear (*Ursus spelaeus*) and cave hyaena (*Crocuta spelaea*) belong to palaeontological findings discovered here. 17 species of bats have been found in the cave with dominating *Rhinolophus ferrumequinum* and *Rhinolophus hipposideros*. The cave is one of the most important winter refuges of these species in Slovakia.

It was inhabited by man in the Neolithic Era („bukovohorská" culture), Bronze Age, Hallstatt and Roman Era. Sporadic findings indicate also a possible short-term Palaeolithic settlement.

The cave was most probably discovered by some of the monks of the nearby Premonstrate Monastery. Its existence was documented already in the second half of the 12th century. The oldest inscription dates back to 1452. Many wall inscriptions of 1571, 1619, 1654, 1655, 1657, 1783, etc. refer to events that had taken place in Jasov and its surroundigs. It is publicly accessible since 1846. After reconstruction it was re-opened for the public in 1924.

It serves for speleotherapeutical procedures since 1995. Currently, 550 m of the cave are open to the public.

DIE HÖHLE JASOVSKÁ

Die Höhle liegt im Hügelland Medzevská pahorkatina an der Schnittstelle zu dem östlichen Rand des Plateaus Jasovská planina im Karstgebiet Slovenský kras, am westlichen Rand der Ortschaft Jasov. Sie liegt in der Nationalen Naturreservation Jasovské dubiny auf dem Territorium des Landschaftsschutzgebietes Biosphärische Reservation Slowakischer Karst. Der Eingang in die Höhle auf dem Ostabhang von Jasovská skala liegt in der Höhe von 257 m ü. d. M.

Sie ist in mitteltriassischen Gutenstein-Dolomiten und in Steinalm-Kalksteinen und Dolomiten der Silica-Decke die tektonischen Störungen durch ehemalige unterirdische Gewässer des Flusses Bodva entlang in fünf Entwicklungsetagen entstanden. Sie erreicht die Länge von 2122 m, die vertikale Spannweite beträgt 55 m.

Die reiche Sinterausfüllung ist durch pagodenförmige Stalagmiten, Stalagnaten, Schilder, Trommel, Röhrchen und andere Formen vertreten.

Die am niedrigsten liegenden Teile der Höhle werden durch Schwankungen des Grundwassers überschwemmt. Das niedrigste Niveau des Seespiegels liegt 7 m unter dem Niveau des Oberflächenstromes des Bodva-Flusses, dessen Gewässer derzeit nicht durch die Höhle fließen.

Zu paläontologischen Entdeckungen gehören Knochen des Höhlenbären (*Ursus spelaeus*) und der Höhlenhyäne (*Crocuta spelaea*). 17 Fledermausarten sind festgestellt. Dominant sind die Großhufeisennase (*Rhinolophus ferrumequinum*) und Kleinhufeisennase (*Rhinolophus hipposideros*). Die Höhle ist eine der wichtigsten Winterquartieren der Großhufeisennasen in der Slowakei.

Besiedelt in Neolithikum (Bukovohorska-Kultur), in der Bronzenzeit, in der Hallstattzeit und der römischen Zeit. Seltene Funde zeugen von einer möglichen kurzfristigen paläolitischen Besiedlung.

Die Höhle wurde wahrscheinlich von einem der Mönche des nicht weit entfernten Prämonstratenser Klosters entdeckt. Ihre Existenz war bereits in der zweiten Hälfte des 12. Jahrhunderts bekannt. Die älteste Aufschrift ist aus dem Jahr 1452. Viele Aufschriften an den Wänden aus den Jahren 1571, 1619, 1654, 1655, 1657, 1783 etc. zeugen über die Ereignisse, die in Jasov und der Umgebung passierten. Zugänglich bereits seit 1846. Nach einigen Änderungen wurde sie für die Öffentlichkeit wieder 1924 zugänglich gemacht.

Seit 1995 werden hier speläoklimatische Kuren durchgeführt. Die Länge der Besichtigungsroute beträgt 550 m.

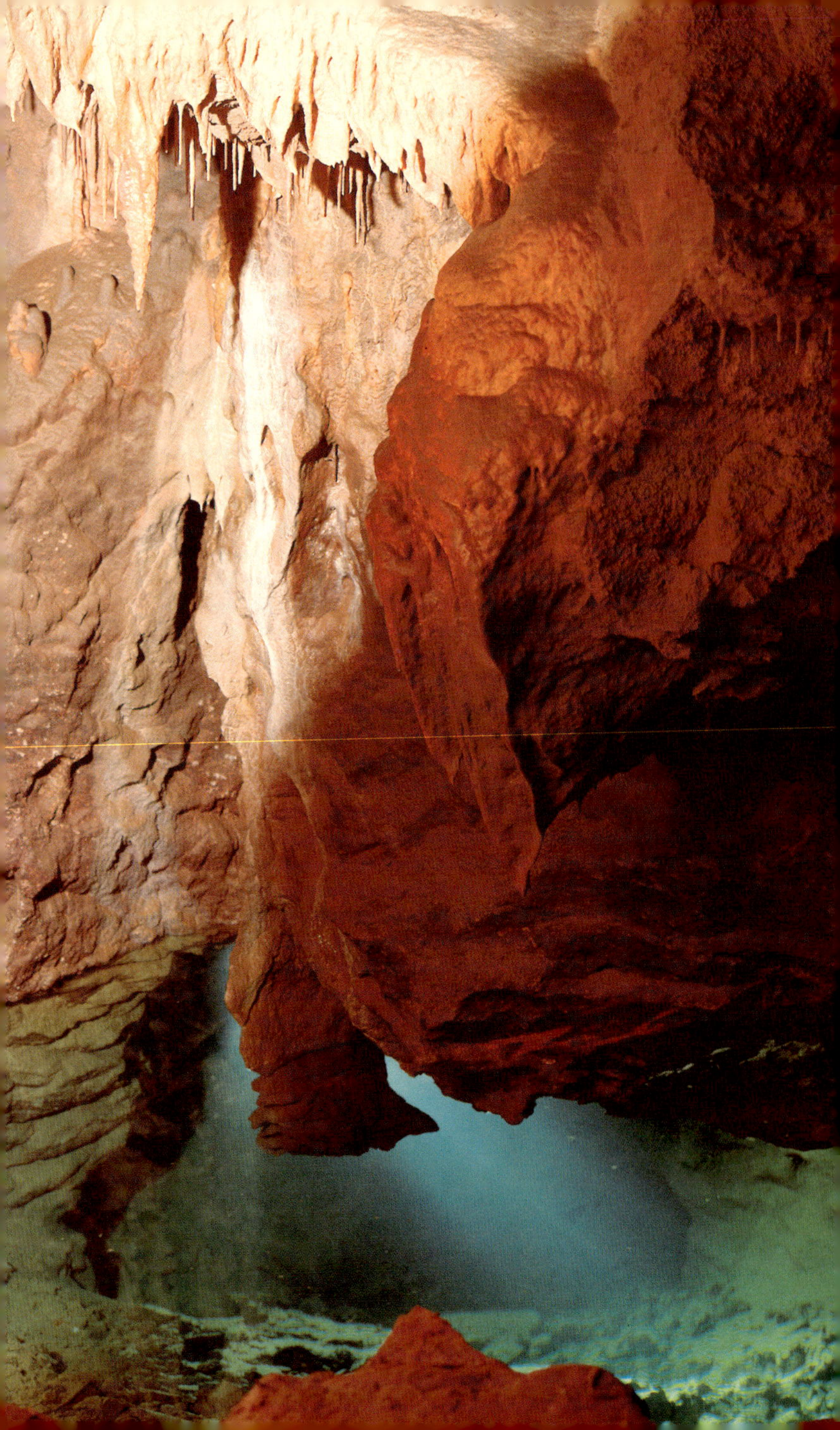

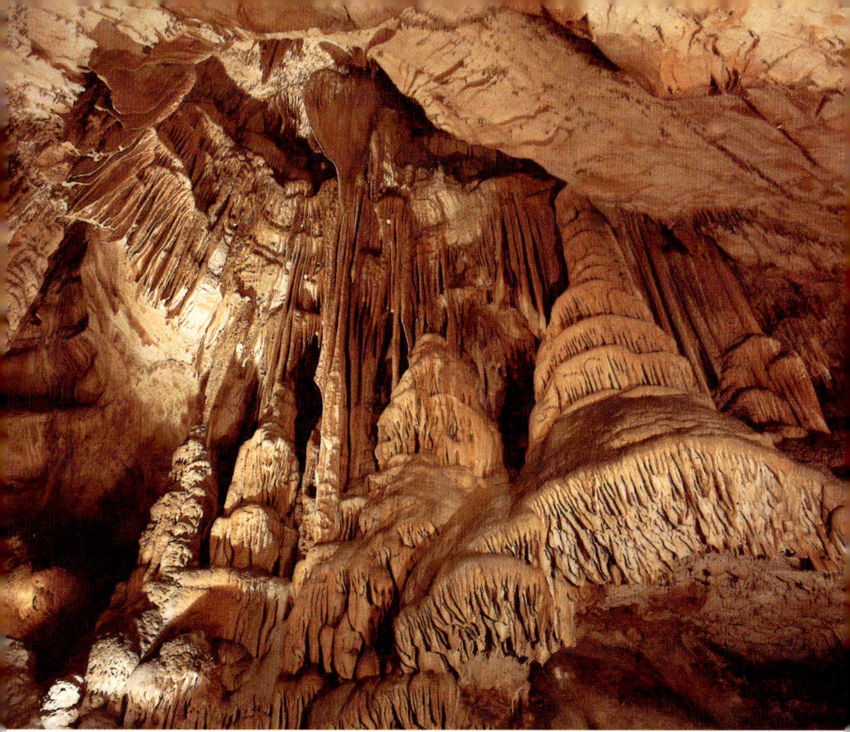

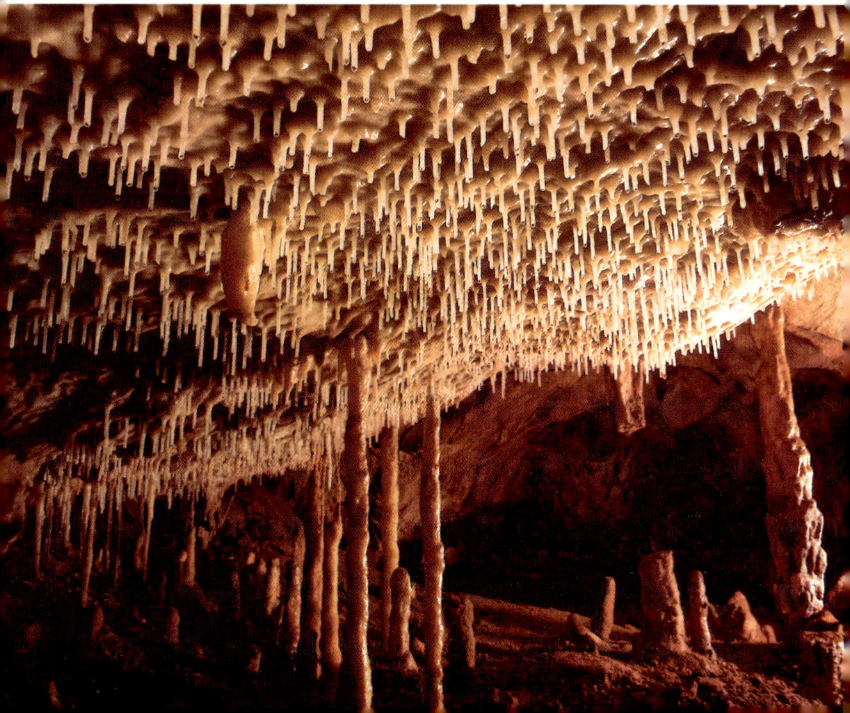

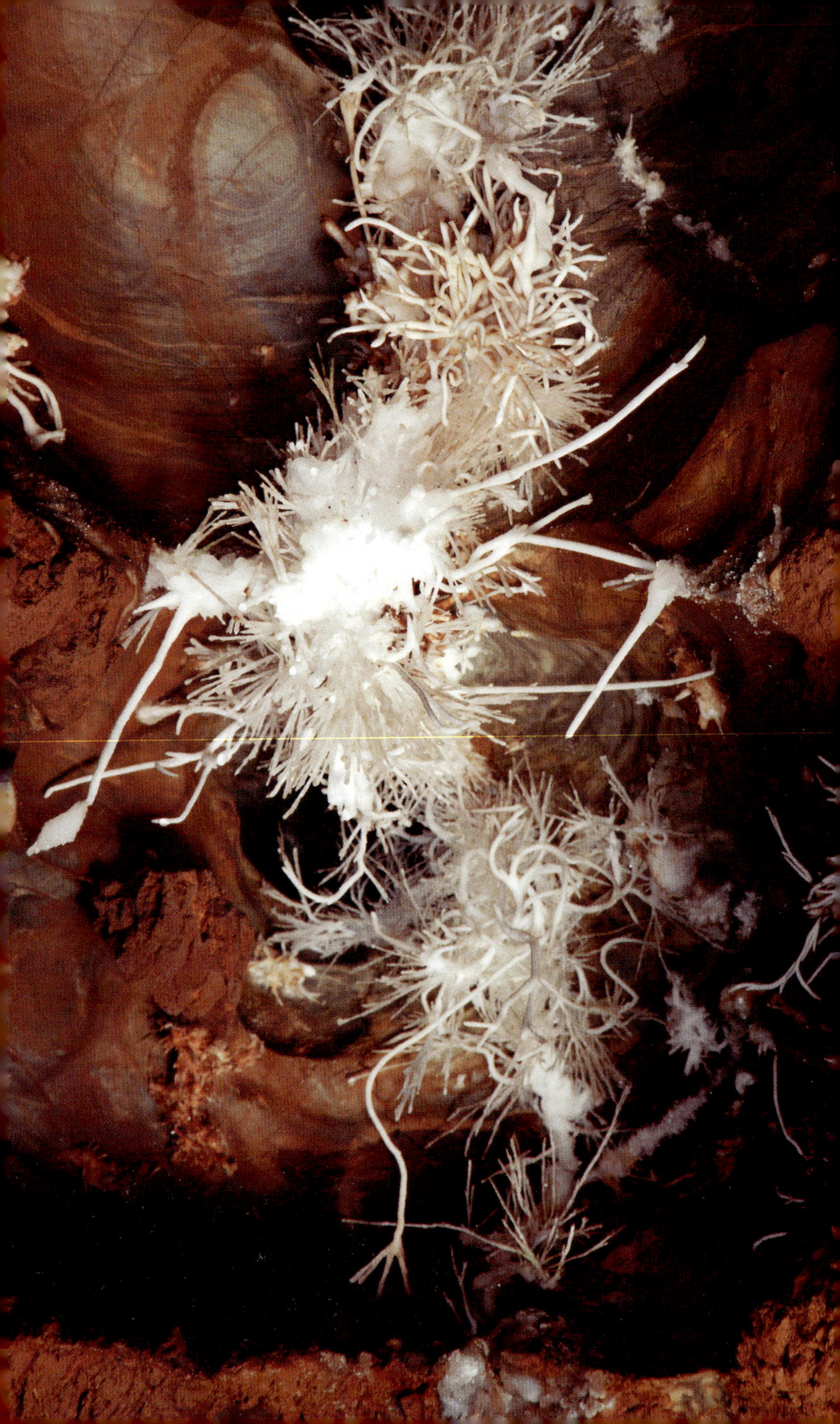

OCHTINSKÁ ARAGONITOVÁ JASKYŇA

NATIONAL NATURE MONUMENT
WORLD NATURAL HERITAGE
NATIONALES NATURDENKMAL
WELTNATURERBE

Cadastral area/Katastergebiet: Ochtiná
District/Kreis: Rožňava
Region/Bezirk: Košice

THE OCHTINSKÁ ARAGONITE CAVE

It is situated in the Ochtinský cryptokarst on the north-western slope of Hrádok Hill in the Revúcka Highland, between Jelšava and Štítnik. Access to the cave is through the 145 m gallery that opens to the cave spaces at 642 m a.s.l. It was formed in a lens of

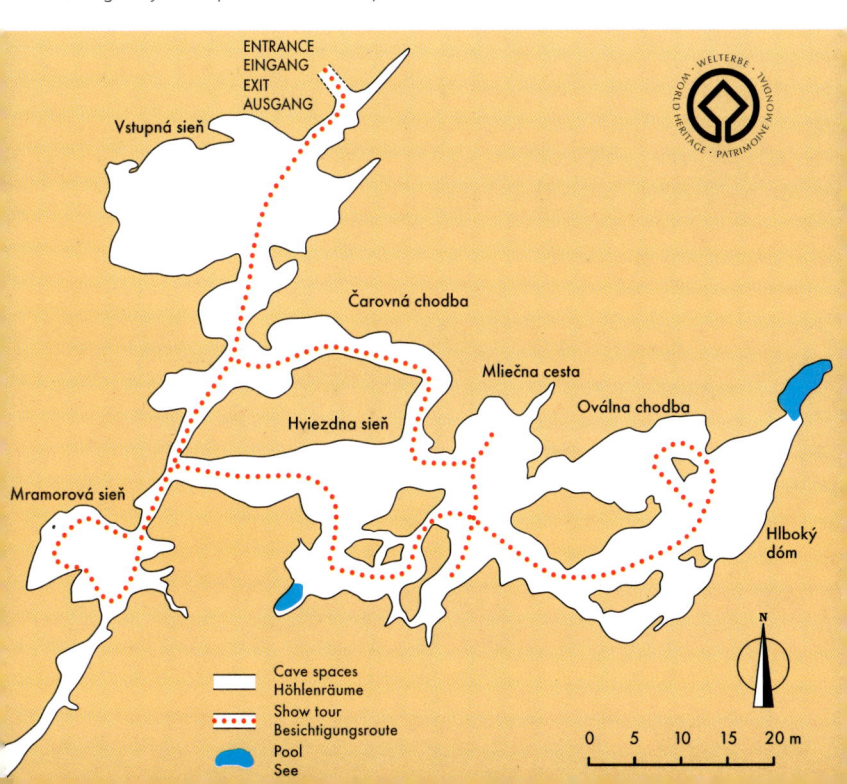

Palaeozoic crystalline limestones (Lower Devonian - Upper Silurian) in Devonian phyllites. A part of the limestones was in the Mesozoic Period in the Upper Cretaceous hydrothermically transformed into ankerites and siderites. The atmospheric water seeping along the tectonic faults caused their weathering and the creation of ochres, that were later flowed away. Overall length of the cave is 300 m. Rich aragonite filling was formed under specific hydrochemical and climatic conditions in closed underground spaces. It occurs in kidney-shaped, needle-shaped and spiral forms. The cave was discovered in 1954 by chance, when driving a new geologic exploratory gallery, by M. Cangár and J. Prošek. It was open to the public in 1972 in the length of 230 m.

DIE ARAGONITHÖHLE OCHTINSKÁ

Die Höhle liegt im Ochtiná-Kryptokarst auf dem nordwestlichen Hügel des Hrádok-Berges im Berggebiet Revúcka vrchovina, zwischen den Ortschaften Jelšava und Štitnik. Die Höhle ist durch einen Stollen von 145 m Länge erschließbar, der in die Höhlenräume in der Höhe von 642 m ü. d. M. mündet. Die Höhle ist in einer Linse der paläozoischen Kristall-Kalksteine (unteres Devon - oberes Silur) in den devonischen Phyliten entstanden. Ein Teil der Kalksteine wandelte im Mesozoikum in oberer Kreide hydrothermal in Ankerite und Siderite. Die durchsickernden atmosphärischen Gewässer die tektonischen Störungen entlang verursachten deren Verwitterung und die Entstehung von Ockern, die später ausgeschwemmt wurden. Die Länge der Höhle beträgt 300 m. Die reiche Aragonitausfüllung entstand unter spezifischen hydrochemischen und klimatischen Verhältnissen in abgeschlossenen unterirdischen Räumen. Sie kommt in Nieren-, Nadel- und Spiralform vor. Die Höhle wurde 1954 bei Vortreiben eines Stollen von Bergarbeitern M. Cangár und J. Prošek zufällig entdeckt. Für Öffentlichkeit sind seit 1972 230 m zugänglich.

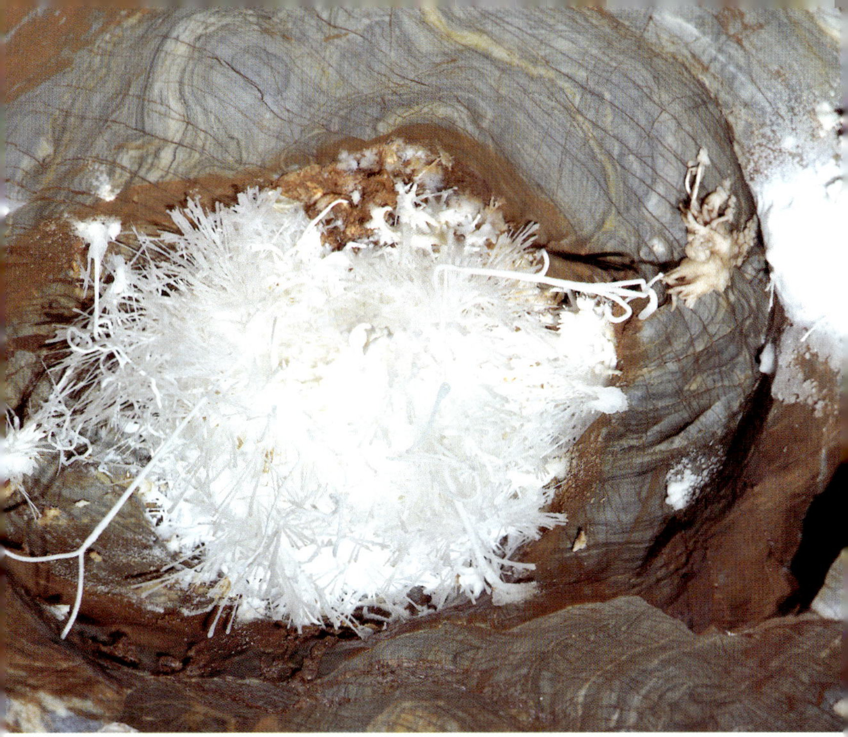

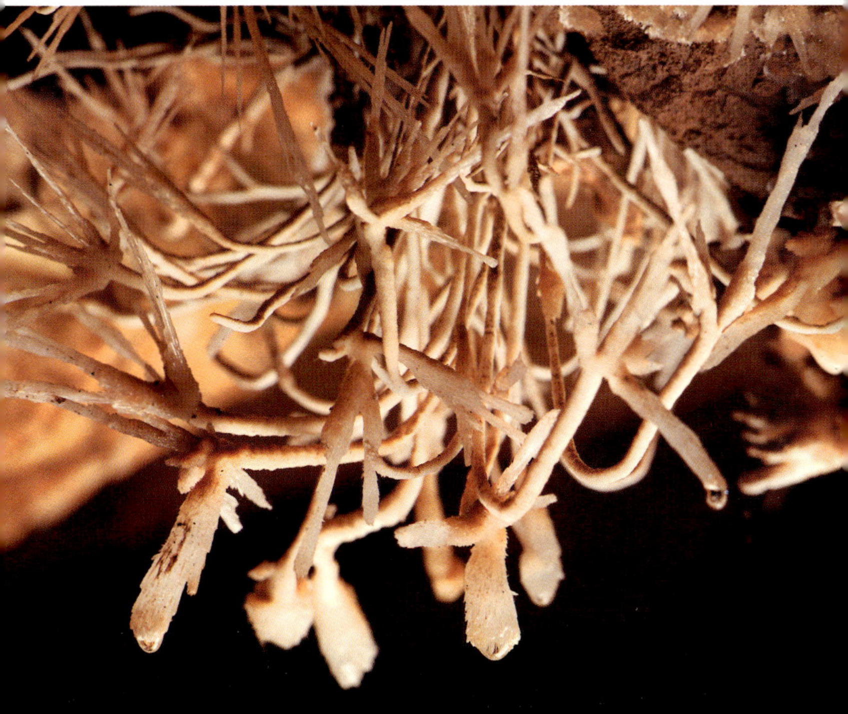

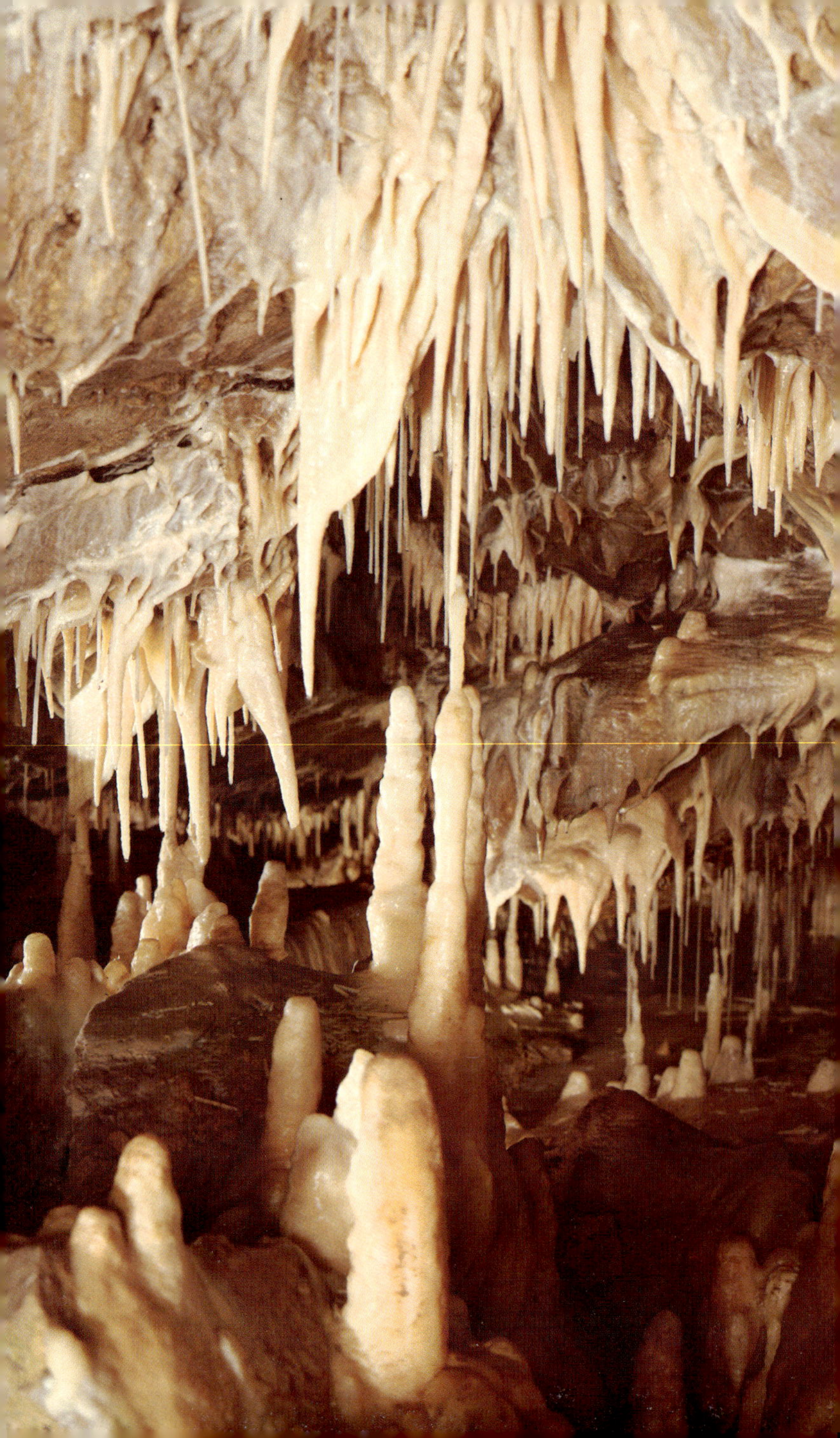

VAŽECKÁ JASKYŇA

NATIONAL NATURE MONUMENT
NATIONALES NATURDENKMAL

Cadastral area/Katastergebiet: Važec
District/Kreis: Liptovský Mikuláš
Region/Bezirk: Žilina

THE VAŽECKÁ CAVE

It is situated in the Važecký Karst at the meeting place of Kozie chrbty (Goat Ranges) with Liptovská Basin, at the western border of Važec, near the main road connecting Liptovský Mikuláš with Poprad - starting points for the tours to the Low and the High Tatras. Entrance to the cave is 784 m a.s.l.

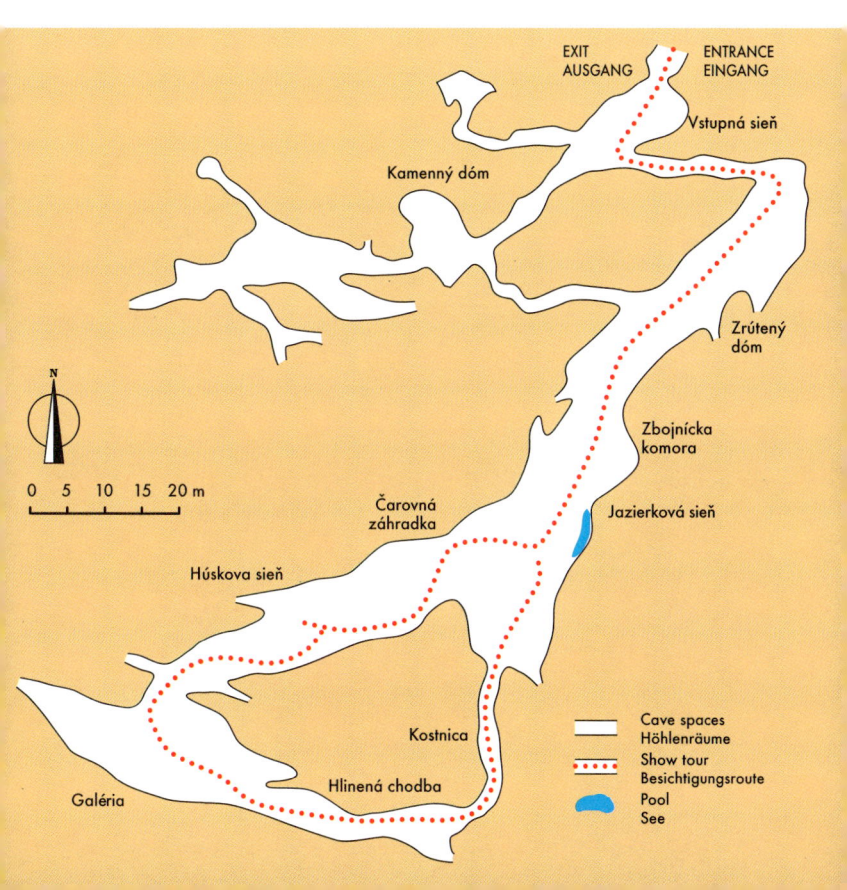

It was formed in the Middle Triassic Gutenstein limestones of Biely Váh series of the Chočský nappe by the former underground waters of the Biely Váh river. The length of the cave is 530 m. The cave spaces are decorated mostly by stalactites, stalagmites and sinter pools. It is an important finding-place of the bones of cave bear (*Ursus spelaeus*).

Entrance hall was long known to the local people. The continuation of cave spaces was discovered by O. A. Húska in 1922. The cave was provisionally opened to the public in 1928. 235 m have been open to the public after reconstruction in 1954.

DIE HÖHLE VAŽECKÁ

Die Höhle befindet sich im Karstgebiet Važecký kras an der Schnittstelle von den Bergen Kozie chrbty mit Liptovská kotlina, am westlichen Rande der Ortschaft Važec, an der Straßenverbindung der Städte Liptovský Mikuláš - Poprad, die Eingangstore in die Niedere und Hohe Tatra sind. Der Eingang in die Höhle liegt 784 m ü. d. M.

Sie ist in mitteltriassischen Gutenstein-Kalksteinen der Biely-Váh-Serie der Choč-Decke durch ehemalige unterirdische Strömungen des Flusses Biely Váh entstanden. Die Höhle ist 530 m lang. Die unterirdischen Räumen sind vor allen von Stalaktiten, Stalagmiten und kleinen Sinterseen dekoriert. Bedeutsame paläontologische Fundstelle der Knochen von Höhlenbären (*Ursus spelaeus*).

Der Eintrittssaal ist den dortigen Einwohnern längst bekannt. Die Fortsetzung der Höhlenräume wurde 1922 von O. A. Húska entdeckt. Im 1928 wurde die Höhle provisorisch zugänglich gemacht. Nach einer Sanierung 1954 sind 235 m zugänglich.

GLOSSARY OF TECHNICAL TERMS
WÖRTERBUCH DER FACHAUSGRÜCKE

Ankerite - a carbonate mineral (Mg, Fe, Mn)Ca(CO$_3$)$_2$.
Aragonite - a carbonate mineral CaCO$_3$, crystallizing in rhombic system.
Bronz Age - a cultural-historical era following the Late Stone Age (in Europe 1900 - 700 years B.C.).
Calcite - a carbonate mineral CaCO$_3$, crystallizing in triangular system.
Cave level of river beds - a horizontal passage of a certain evolutional stage formed by underground water stream dependen on the erosion basis of a karst spring.
Corrosion - dissociation and solution of solid rocks through chemical effects of water and soluble acids.
Cretaceous - the Late Mesozoic Era (130-65 million years ago).
Cryptokarst - a true folded karst rocks covered with non-karst rocks without any signs of karstification on the surface.
Devonian - the Late Palaeozoic (about 400-350 mil. years ago).
Dolomite - a carbonate mineral CaMg(CO)$_2$, in nature it forms huge masses of rock of which the whole basement of mountains are built.
Eddy holes (karst springs) - a place where the underground waters (streams) spring to the surface of karst territories.
Fold - wave-shaped folding of rock beds of the Earth's crust due to lateral pressures.
Hallstatt Era - a cultural-historical era of evolution of mankind (in East Slovakia 700 - 300 years B.C.).
High-mountain karst - a karst landscape of high elevations above the upper forest border.
Horst - tectonic elevation of the terrain due to mountain-forming processes at fault disturbances of the Earth crust.
Interbed surface (bedding joint) - a basic feature of sedimentary rocks separating from each other the later and the earlier bed, formed primarily by rock sedimentation.
Jurassic - the Middle Mesozoic Era (205 - 130 million years ago).
Karst of monoclinal crests - slantly positioned complex of karst rocks with steep slopes on the frontal parts of the bed and milder slopes along the interbed surfaces.
Limestone - a sedimentary rock composed of calcium carbonate, calcite.
Nappe - a faultblock of the Earth's crust shifted and laid on other layers through lateral pressure due to mountain-forming processes.
Neolith - the Late Stone Age, falls into the Middle Holocene in the Late Quaternary (beginning in 9th millenium B.C.).
Ochre - iron hydroxide product of oxidation of iron bound in ankerite.
Palaeolith - the Early Stone Age, the oldest era of human history - in Early Quaternary Late Palaeolith 600-150 thousand years ago, Middle Palaeolith 150-40 thousand years ago, Early Palaeolith 40-15 thousand years ago.
Ponor (swallow hole) - the place where the surface water streams are disappearing into the underground in karst territories.
Roman Era - a cultural-historical era in evolution of mankind following the Laten Era (0-400 y. A.D.).
Siderite - a carbonate mineral FeCO$_3$.
Silurian - the Early Palaeozoic (about 420-400 million years ago).
Sinter - a crystalline or amorphous sediment from the flowing solutions; flowstone - a calcite sinter that forms frequently the filling of cave spaces (dripstones and other formations).
Sinter drum - a formation created by growing stalactite forms at the circumference of sinter shield.
Sinter shield - a thin, oval, disc, flat sinter crust hanging from the cave's wall in slant or horizontal position; some shields have been formed on the former river sediments, later washed away in younger developmental phase of the cave.
Sinter waterfall - a massive influx of sinter on the cave's wall precipitated from the flowing water.
Speleoclimatic procedures - usage of climatic conditions in caves for curative courses.
Speleotherapy - the treatment of the diseases of upper airways and allergies through beneficial effects of the climatic conditions (aerosol) in cave spaces.
Stalactite - a dripstone formation hanging from the ceiling of the cave space created through the precipitation of sinter of the downflowing water.
Stalagmite - a dripstone formation growing up from bottom of the cave space through the precipitation sinter of the water drops falling down from above.
Stalagnate - a dripstone column from the ceiling to the floor of the cave space created through the meeting of stalactite and stalagmite.
Tectonic faults - deformation of the rocks due to the movement of the Earth's crust during mountain-forming processes.
Travertine, tuff - sedimentary rock formed by the precipitation of calcium carbonate from the fresh water solutions.
Triassic - the earliest period of Mesozoic Era and the corresponding system of rocks (about 245 - 205 million years ago).

Ankerit - Karbonatmineral (Mg, Fe, Mn)Ca(CO$_3$)$_2$.
Aragonit - Karbonatmineral CaCO$_3$, kristallisiert im Rhombussystem.
Bronzenzeit - kultur-historische Periode in der Menschheitsentwicklung nach der jüngeren Steinzeit (in Europa 1900 - 700 Jahre v.u.Z.).
Decke - eine durch Wirkung gebirgebildender Prozesse infolge des Seitendruckes auf andere Schichten verschobene und aufschobene Erdkrustescholle.
Devon - Formation des Paläozoikums (ca. vor 400 - 350 Mio. Jahren).
Dolomit - Karbonatmineral CaMg(CO$_3$)$_2$, in der Natur bildet er riesige Gesteinemasse, aus denen ganze Gebirgszüge bestehen.
Falte - wellenförmige Biegung der Gesteinschichten der Erdkruste bei gebirgebildenden Prozessen infolge seitlichen Druckes.
Hallstattzeit - kultur-historische Periode in der Menschheitsentwicklung nach der Bronzenzeit (in der Ostslowakei 700 - 300 Jahre v.u.Z.).
Hochgebirgskarst - Karstgebiet in hohen Lagen über der oberen Waldgrenze.
Höhlenniveau der Flußbetten - horizontaler Gang eines bestimmten Entwicklungsstadiums, gebildet durch unter irdischen Wasserfluß in Abhängigkeit von der Erosionsbasis des Karstquelle.
Horst - gehobene tektonische Geländeform, gebildet bei gebirgebildenden Prozessen bei den Bruchstörungen der Erdkrusten.
Jura - mittlere Formation des Mesozoikums (vor 205 - 130 Mio. Jahren).
Kalkstein - Sedimentgestein aus Kalziumoxid, Kalzit.
Kalzit - Karbonatmineral CaCO$_3$, kristallisiert im Dreieck-System.
Karst der monoklinen Bergrücken - querliegender Komplex von Karstgesteinen mit steifen Abhängen auf den Schichtenstirnflächen und mäßigen Abhängen entlang den Schichtenflächen.
Karstquelle - Ort, wo unterirdische Wasser, oft unterirdische Wasserflüsse auf die Oberfläche im Karstgebieten quellen.
Korrosion - Auflösung fester Gesteine durch chemische Wirkung von Wasser und den aufgelösten Säuren.
Kreide - die jüngste Formation des Mesozoikums (vor 130 - 65 Mio. Jahren).
Kryptokarst - Lagen der Kartsgesteine, gefaltet und überzogen mit Nicht-Karstgesteinen ohne Verkarstungerscheinungen an der Oberfläche.
Neolithikum - jüngere Steinzeit, gehört in die Formation des mittleren Holozäns im jüng. Quartär (Anfänge im 9. Jh. v.u.Z.)
Oker - Eisenhydroxid, Produkt der Oxidation des in Ankerit gebundenen Eisens.
Paläolithikum - ältere Steinzeit, älteste Periode der menschheitsgeschichte im älteren Quartär (älteres Paläolithikum vor 600 - 150 Tsd. Jahren, mittleres Paläolithikum vor 150 - 40 Tsd. Jahren, jüngeres Paläolithikum 40 - 15 Tsd. Jahren).
Römische Zeit - kultur-historische Periode in der Menschheitsentwicklung nach der La-Téne-Zeit (0 - 400 Jahre u. Z.).
Schichtenzwischenfläche - Basismerkmal der Sedimentgesteine, trennt die ältere und jüngere Schicht ab; primär bei Gesteineablagerung gebildet.
Siderit - karbonatisches Eisenerz FeCO$_3$.
Silur - erdgeschichtliche Formation des Paläozoikums (ca. vor 420 - 400 Mio. Jahren).
Sinter - kristalline oder amorphe Ablagerung aus den umlaufenden Lösungen; der Kalksinter bildet oft die Ausfüllung der Höhlenräume (Tropfsteine und andere Formen).
Sinterschild - ovale dünne und flache aus der Höhlenwand schräg oder waagerecht hängende Sinterkruste; einige Schilder sind auf ehemaligen, später abgeschwemmten Flußsedimenten in der jüngeren Entwicklungsphase der Höhle gebildet worden.
Sintertrommel - ein durch Aufwachsen der Stalaktitformen auf der Umleitung des Sinterschildes entstandenes Gebilde.
Sinterwasserfall - massiver Überzug des an der Höhlenwand aus dem fließenden Wasser kondensierten Sinters.
Spelöklimatische Kuren - Heilprozeduren in den Höhlenräumen.
Speläotherapie - Heilverfahren bei Erkrankungen oberer Atemwege und Alergien mit Nützung der günstigen klimatischen Bedingungen - des Aerosols - in den Höhlen.
Stalagmit - Tropfstein, der vom Boden der Höhle nach oben wächst und durch Sinterausscheidung des fallenden und spritzenden Wassers entsteht.
Stalagnat - Tropfsteinsäule vom Boden bis zur Decke der Höhle, die durch Verbinden vom Stalagmit und Stalaktit entstanden ist.
Stalaktit - Tropfstein, der von der Höhlendecke nach unten wächst und durch Sinterausscheidung der Tropfen entsteht.
Tektonische Störungen - Erscheinungen der Gesteinedeformationen infolge der Bewegung der Erdkruste bei gebirgebildenden Prozessen.
Travertin - Sedimentgestein, das durch Ausscheidung des Kalziumkarbides aus Süßwasserlösungen entsteht.
Trias - älteste Formation des Mesozoikums (ca. vor 245 - 205 Mio. Jahren).
Wasserschwinde - Stelle, wo die fließende Oberflächengewässer in das Unterirdische im Karstgebiet verschwinden.

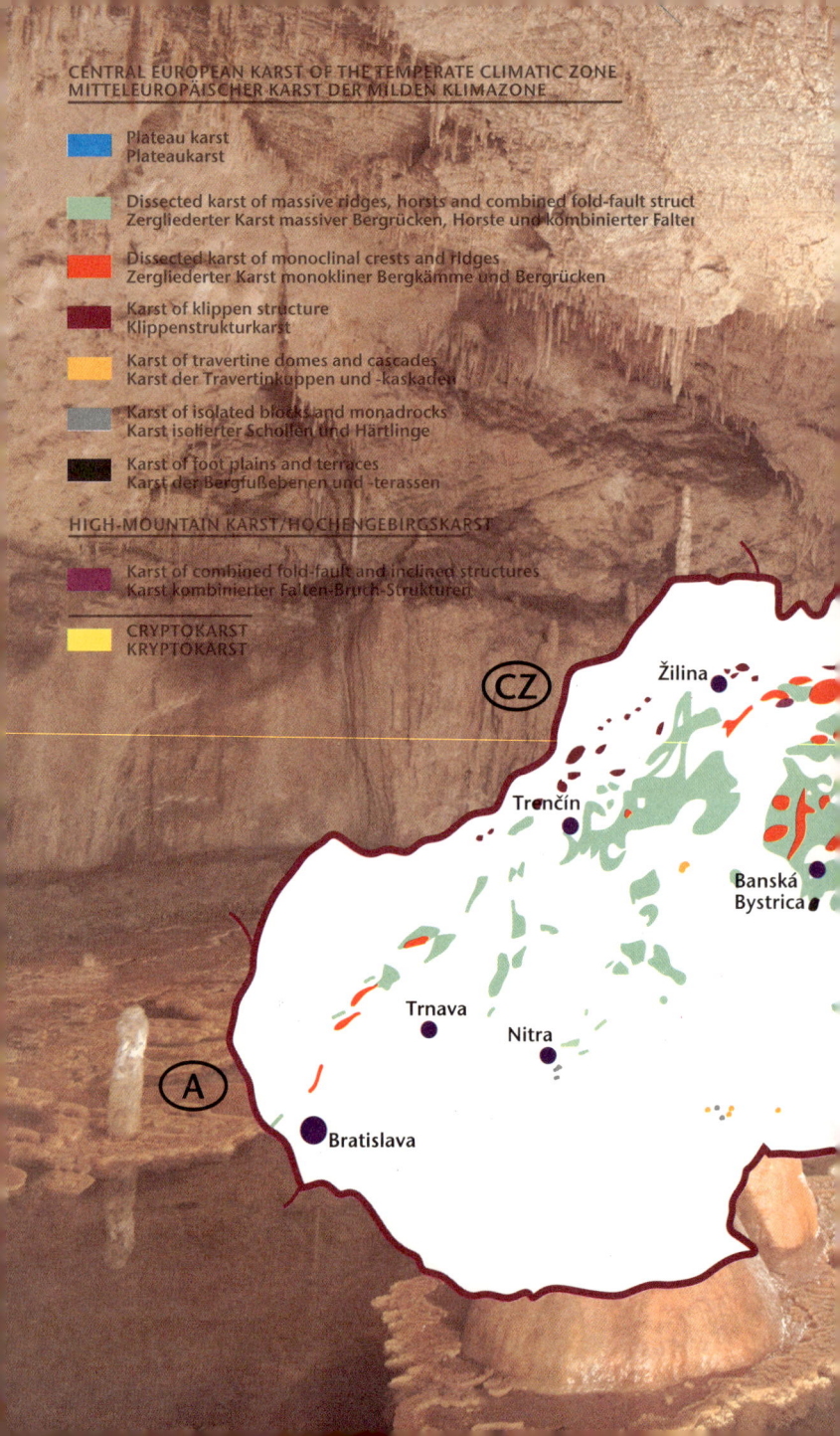

CENTRAL EUROPEAN KARST OF THE TEMPERATE CLIMATIC ZONE
MITTELEUROPÄISCHER KARST DER MILDEN KLIMAZONE

- Plateau karst / Plateaukarst
- Dissected karst of massive ridges, horsts and combined fold-fault struct... / Zergliederter Karst massiver Bergrücken, Horste und kombinierter Falten...
- Dissected karst of monoclinal crests and ridges / Zergliederter Karst monokliner Bergkämme und Bergrücken
- Karst of klippen structure / Klippenstrukturkarst
- Karst of travertine domes and cascades / Karst der Travertinkuppen und -kaskaden
- Karst of isolated blocks and monadrocks / Karst isolierter Schollen und Härtlinge
- Karst of foot plains and terraces / Karst der Bergfußebenen und -terassen

HIGH-MOUNTAIN KARST / HOCHENGEBIRGSKARST

- Karst of combined fold-fault and inclined structures / Karst kombinierter Falten-Bruch-Strukturen

CRYPTOKARST / KRYPTOKARST